PREFACE.

THE Receipts composing the Volume here submitted to the Public have been collected under peculiarly favourable circumstances by a Lady of distinction, whose productions in the lighter department of literature entitle her to a place among the most successful writers of the present day. Moving in the first circles of rank and fashion, her associations have qualified her to furnish directions adapted to the manners and taste of the most refined Luxury; whilst long and attentive observation, and the communications of an extensive acquaintance, have enabled her equally to accommodate them to the use of persons of less ample means and of simpler and more economical habits.

When the task of arranging the mass of materials thus accumulated devolved upon the Editor, it became his study to give to them such a form as should be most convenient for constant reference. A glance at the "Contents," which might with equal propriety be denominated an Index, will, he flatters himself, convince the reader that this object has been accomplished. It will there be seen that the Receipts, upwards of SIXTEEN HUNDRED in number, are classed under Eleven distinct Heads, each of which is arranged in alphabetical order—a method which confers on this Volume a decided advantage over every other work of the kind, inasmuch as it affords all the facilities of a Dictionary, without being liable to the unpleasant intermixture of heterogeneous matters which cannot be avoided in that form of arrangement.

The intimate connexion between the Science of Cookery and the Science of Health, the sympathies subsisting between every part of the system and the stomach, and the absolute necessity of strict attention not less to the manner of preparing the alimentary substances offered to that organ than to their quality and quantity, have been of late years so repeatedly and so forcibly urged by professional pens, that there needs no argument here to prove the utility of a safe Guide and Director in so important a department of domestic economy as that which is the subject of this Volume. In many more cases, indeed, than the uninitiated would imagine, is the healthy tone of the stomach dependent on the proper preparation of the food, the healthy tone of the body in general on that of the stomach, and the healthy tone of the mind on that of the body: consequently the first of these conditions ought to command the vigilance and solicitude of all who are desirous of securing the true enjoyment of life—the *mens sana in corpore sano*.

The professed Cook may perhaps be disposed to form a mean estimate of these pages, because few, or no learned, or technical, terms are employed in them; but this circumstance, so far from operating to the disparagement of the work, must prove a strong recommendation to the Public in general. The chief aim, in fact, of the noble Authoress has been to furnish such plain directions, in every branch of the culinary art, as shall be really useful to English masters and English servants, and to the humble but earnest practitioner. Let those who may desire to put this collection of receipts to the test only give them a fair trial, neither trusting to conceited servants, who, despising all other methods, obstinately adhere to their own, and then lay the blame of failure upon the directions; nor committing their execution to careless ones, who neglect the means prescribed for success, either in regard to time, quantities, or cleanliness; and the result will not fail to afford satisfactory evidence of their pleasant qualities and practical utility.

GENERAL DIRECTIONS.

The following directions may appear trite and common, but it is of the greatest consequence that they be strictly observed:

Attend to minute cleanliness. Never wipe a dish, bowl, or pan, with a half dirty napkin, or give the vessel a mere rinse in water and think that it is then fit for use. See that it be dried and pure from all smell before you put in any ingredient.

Never use the hands when it is possible to avoid it; and, when you do, have a clean basin of water to dip them in, and wipe them thoroughly several times while at work, as in mixing dough, &c.

Use silver or wooden spoons; the latter are best for all confectionery and puddings. Take care that the various spoons, skewers, and knives, be not used promiscuously for cookery and confectionery, or even for different dishes of the same sort.

If an onion is cut with any knife, or lies near any article of kitchen use, that article is not fit for service till it has been duly scoured and laid in the open air. The same remark applies to very many strong kitchen herbs. This point is scarcely ever enough attended to.

In measuring quantities, be extremely exact, having always some particular vessel set apart for each ingredient (best of earthenware, because such cannot retain any smell) wherewith to ascertain your quantities. Do nothing by guess, how practised soever you may deem yourself in the art: nor say "Oh! I want none of your measures for such a thing as a little seasoning," taking a pinch here and there. Be assured you will never in that way make a dish, or a sauce, twice in the same manner; it may be good by *chance*, but it will always be a *chance*, and the chances are very much against it; at all events it will not be precisely the *same* thing, and precision is the very essence of good cookery.

The French say *Il faut que rien ne domine*—No one ingredient must predominate. This is a good rule to please general taste and great judges; but, to secure the favour of a particular palate it is not infallible: as, in a good herb soup, for instance, it may better delight the master or mistress that some one herb or savoury meat *should* predominate. Consult, therefore, the peculiarities of the tastes of your employer; for, though a dish may be a good dish of its kind, if it is not suited to the taste of the eater of what avail is it?

Let not the vanity of the cook induce you to forget the duty of a servant, which is, in the first place, to please his master: be particular, therefore, in enquiring what things please your employer. Many capital cooks will be found for great feasts and festivals, but very few for every-day service, because this is not "eye-service," but the service of principle and duty. Few, indeed, there are who will take equal pains to make one delicate dish, one small exquisite dinner, for the three hundred and sixty-five days in the year; yet this is by far the most valuable attainment of the two.

The great secret of all cookery consists in making fine meat jellies; this is done at less expence than may be imagined by a *careful, honest* cook. For this purpose let all parings of meats of every kind, all bones, however dry they may appear, be carefully collected, and put over a very slow fire in a small quantity of water, always adding a little more as the water boils down. Skim this juice when cool: and, having melted it a second time, pass it through a sieve till thoroughly pure: put no salt or pepper; use this fine jelly for any sauce, adding herbs, or whatever savoury condiments you think proper, at the time it is used.

Be careful all summer long to dry vegetables and herbs. Almost every herb and vegetable may be dried and preserved for winter use; for on these must chiefly depend all the varied flavours of your dishes. Mushrooms and artichokes strung on a string, with a bit of wood knotted in between each to prevent their touching, and hung in a dry place, will be excellent; and every species of culinary herb may be preserved either in bottles or paper bags.

GENERAL RULES FOR A GOOD DINNER.

There should be always two soups, white and brown, two fish, dressed and undressed; a bouilli and petits-patés; and on the sideboard a plain roast joint, besides many savoury articles, such as hung beef, Bologna sausages, pickles, cold ham, cold pie, &c. some or all of these according to the number of guests, the names of which the head-servant ought to whisper about to the company, occasionally offering them. He should likewise carry about all the side-dishes or *entrées*, after the soups are taken away in rotation. A silver lamp should be kept burning, to put any dish upon that may grow cold.

It is indispensable to have candles, or plateau, or epergne, in the middle of the table.

Beware of letting the table appear loaded; neither should it be too bare. The soups and fish should be dispatched before the rest of the dinner is set on; but, lest any of the guests eat of neither, two small dishes of patés should be on the table. Of course, the meats and vegetables and fruits which compose these dinners must be varied according to the season, the number of guests, and the tastes of the host and hostess. It is also needless to add that without iced champagne and Roman punch a dinner is not called a dinner.

These observations and the following directions for dinners are suitable to persons who chuse to live *fashionably*; but the receipts contained in this book will suit any mode of living, and the persons consulting it will find matter for all tastes and all establishments. There is many an excellent dish not considered adapted to a fashionable table, which, nevertheless, is given in these pages.

SOUPS.

Almond Soup.

TAKE lean beef or veal, about eight or nine pounds, and a scrag of mutton; boil them gently in water that will cover them, till the gravy be very strong and the meat very tender; then strain off the gravy and set it on the fire with two ounces of vermicelli, eight blades of mace, twelve cloves, to a gallon. Let it boil till it has the flavour of the spices. Have ready one pound of the best almonds, blanched and pounded very fine; pound them with the yolks of twelve eggs, boiled hard, mixing as you pound them with a little of the soup, lest the almonds should grow oily. Pound them till they are a mere pulp: add a little soup by degrees to the almonds and eggs until mixed together. Let the soup be cool when you mix it, and do it perfectly smooth. Strain it through a sieve; set it on the fire; stir it frequently; and serve it hot. Just before you take it up add a gill of thick cream.

Asparagus Soup.

Put five or six pounds of lean beef, cut in pieces and rolled in flour, into your stewpan, with two or three slices of bacon at the bottom: set it on a slow fire and cover it close, stirring it now and then, till your gravy is drawn; then put in two quarts of water and half a pint of pale ale; cover it close and let it stew gently for an hour. Put in some whole pepper and salt to your taste. Then strain out the liquor and take off the fat; put in the leaves of white beet, some spinach, some cabbage lettuce, a little mint, sorrel, and sweet marjoram, pounded; let these boil up in your liquor. Then put in your green tops of asparagus, cut small, and let them boil till all is tender. Serve hot, with the crust of a French roll in the dish.

Another.

Boil three half pints of winter split peas; rub them through a sieve; add a little gravy; then stew by themselves the following herbs:—celery, a few young onions, a lettuce, cut small, and about half a pint of asparagus, cut small, like peas, and stewed with the rest; colour the soup of a pea green with spinach juice; add half a pint of cream or good milk, and serve up.

Calf's Head Soup.

Take a knuckle of veal, and put as much water to it as will make a good soup; let it boil, skimming it very well. Add two carrots, three anchovies, a little mace, pepper, celery, two onions, and some sweetherbs. Let it boil to a good soup, and strain it off. Put to it a full half pint of Madeira wine; take a good many mushrooms, stew them in their own liquor; add this sauce to your soup. Scald the calf's head as for a hash; cut it in the same manner, but smaller; flour it a little, and fry it of a fine brown. Then put the soup and fried head together into a stewpan, with some oysters and mushrooms, and let them stew gently for an hour.

Carrot Soup.

Take about two pounds of veal and the same of lean beef; make it into a broth or gravy, and put it by until wanted. Take a quarter of a pound of butter, four large fine carrots, two turnips, two parsnips, two heads of celery, and four onions; stew these together about two hours, and shake it often that they may not burn to the stewpan; then add the broth made as above, boiling hot, in quantity to your own judgment, and as you like it for thickness. It should be of about the consistency of pea-soup. Pass it through a tamis. Season to your taste.

Another.

Take four pounds of beef, a scrag of mutton, about a dozen large carrots, four onions, some pepper and salt; put them into a gallon of water, and boil very gently for four hours. Strain the meat, and take the carrots and rub them very smooth through a hair sieve, adding the gravy by degrees till about as thick as cream. The gravy must have all the fat taken off before it is added to the carrots. Turnip soup is made in the same way.

Clear Soup.

Take six pounds of gravy beef; cut it small, put it into a large stewpan, with onions, carrots, turnips, celery, a small bunch of herbs, and one cup of water. Stew these on the fire for an hour, then add nine pints of boiling water; let it boil for six hours, strain it through a fine sieve, and let it stand till next day; take off the fat; put it into a clean stewpan, set it on the fire till it is quite hot; then break three eggs into a basin, leaving the shells with them. Add this to the soup by degrees; cover close till it boils; then strain it into a pan through a fine cloth. When the eggs are well beaten, a little hot soup must be added by degrees, and beaten up before it is put into the stewpan with the whole of the soup.

Clear Herb Soup.

Put celery, leeks, carrots, turnips, cabbage lettuce, young onions, all cut fine, with a handful of young peas: give them a scald in boiling water; put them on a sieve to drain, and then put them into a clear consommé, and let them boil slowly till the roots are quite tender. Season with a little salt. When going to table put a little crust of French roll in it.

Cod's Head Soup.

Take six large onions, cut them in slices, and put them in a stewpan, with a quarter of a pound of the freshest butter. Set it in a stove to simmer for an hour, covered up close; take the head, and with a knife and fork pick all the fins you can get off the fish. Put this in a dish, dredge it well with flour, and let it stand. Take all the bones of the head and the remainder, and boil them on the fire for an hour, with an English pint of water. Strain off the liquor through a sieve, and put it to your onions; take a good large handful of parsley, well washed and picked clean; chop it as fine as possible; put it in the soup; let it just boil, otherwise it will make it yellow. Add a little cayenne pepper, two spoonfuls of anchovy, a little soy, a little of any sort of ketchup, and a table-spoonful of vinegar. Then put the fish that has been set aside on the plate into the stewpan to the soup, and let it simmer for ten minutes. If not thick enough add a small piece of butter rolled in flour.

Crawfish Soup.

Boil off your crawfish; take the tails out of the shells; roast a couple of lobsters; beat these with your crawfish shells; put this into your fish stock, with some crusts of French rolls. Rub the whole through a tamis, and put your tails into it. You may farce a carp and put in the middle, if you please, or farce some of the shells and stick on a French roll.

Crawfish, or Lobster Soup.

Take some middling and small fishes, and put them in a gallon of water, with pepper, salt, cloves, mace, sweetherbs, and onions; boil them to pieces, and strain them out of the liquor. Then take a large fish, cut the flesh off one side, make forcemeat of it, and lay it on the fish; dredge grated bread in it, and butter a dish well; put it in the oven and bake it. Then take one hundred crawfish, break the shells of the tails and claws, take out the meat as whole as you can; pound the shells and add the spawn of a lobster pounded; put them into the soup, and, if you like, a little veal gravy; give them a boil or two together. Strain the liquor off into another saucepan, with the tops of French bread, dried, beat fine, and sifted. Give it a boil to thicken; then brown some butter, and put in the tails and claws of the crawfish, and some of the forcemeat made into balls. Lay the baked fish in the middle of the dish, pour the soup boiling hot on it; if you like, add yolks of eggs, boiled hard, pounded, and mixed by degrees with the soup.

Curry or Mulligatawny Soup.

Boil a large chicken or fowl in a pint of water till half done; add a table-spoonful of curry powder, with the juice of one lemon and a half; boil it again gently till the meat is done.

For a large party you must double the quantity of all the articles, and always proportion the water to the quantity of gravy you think the meat will yield.

Eel Soup.

Take two pounds of eels; put to them two quarts of water, a crust of bread, two or three blades of mace, some whole pepper, one onion, and a bunch of sweet herbs. Cover them close, and let them stew till the liquor is reduced to one half, and if the soup is not rich enough it must boil till it is stronger.—Then strain it, toast some bread, and cut it in small.

This soup will be as good as if meat were put into it. A pound of eels makes a pint of soup.

Fish Soup.

Stew the heads, tails, and fins, of any sort of flat fish or haddock. Strain and thicken with a little flour and butter; add pepper, salt, anchovy, and ketchup, to taste. Cut the fish in thick pieces, and let them stew gently till done.

French Soup.

Take the scrag end of a neck of mutton, or two pounds of any meat, and make it into very strong broth; then take one large cabbage, three lettuces, three carrots, one root of celery, and two onions; cut them all small, and fry them with butter. Pour your broth upon your vegetables a little at a time, cover it up close, and let it stew three hours or more. Serve with the vegetables.

Friar's Chicken.

Stew a knuckle of veal, a neck of mutton, a large fowl, two pounds of giblets, two large onions, two bunches of turnips, one bunch of carrots, a bunch of thyme, and another of sage, eight hours over a very slow stove, till every particle of juice is extracted from the meat and vegetables. Take it off the stove, pass it through a hair tamis; have ready a pound of grated veal, or, what is better, of grated chicken, with a large bunch of parsley, chopped very fine and mingled with it. Put this into the broth; set it on the stove again, and while there break four raw eggs into it. Stir the whole for about a quarter of an hour and serve up hot.

Giblet Soup. No. 1.

Take the desired quantity of strong beef gravy; add to it a few slices of veal fried in butter; take a piece of butter rolled in flour, and with it fry some sliced onion and thyme; when made brown, add it to the soup. When sufficiently stewed, strain and put to it two spoonfuls of ketchup, a few spoonfuls of Madeira, and a little lemon juice. The giblets being separately stewed in a pint of water, add their gravy to the soup.

Giblet Soup. No. 2.

Parboil the giblets, and pour the water from them; put them into fresh water or thin gravy, with a large onion stuck with cloves; season it to your taste; boil them till the flesh comes from the bones. Mix the yolk of an egg with flour into a paste; roll it two or three times over with a rollingpin; cut it in pieces, and thicken the soup with it.

Giblet Soup. No. 3.

Take three pair of goose giblets; scald and cut them as for stewing; set them on the fire in three quarts of water, and when the scum rises skim them well: put in a bundle of sweet herbs, some cloves, mace, and allspice, tied in a bag, with some pepper and salt. Stew them very gently till nearly tender: mix a quarter of a pound of butter with flour, and put it in, with half a pint of white wine, and a little cayenne pepper. Stew them till thick and smooth; take out the herbs and spices; skim well; boil the livers in a quart of water till tender, and put in. Serve up in a terrine or dish.

Gravy Soup. No. 1.

Put two pounds of gravy beef, cut in small pieces, with pepper, salt, some whole pepper, and a piece of butter, the size of a walnut, into a stewpan. When drawn to a good gravy, pour in three quarts of boiling water; add some mace, four heads of celery, one carrot, and three or four onions. Let them stew gently about an hour and a half; then strain; add an ounce and half of vermicelli, and let it stew about ten minutes longer.

Gravy Soup. No. 2.

Take two ox melts, cut them in pieces, season them with pepper and salt, and dredge them with flour. Shred two large onions, fry them of a nice brown colour, put them at the bottom of the saucepan with a piece of butter. Take one ox rump, stew it with carrots and celery and twelve allspice. Then put all together and strain well. This quantity will make three quarts. You may send the ox rump to table in the soup, if approved. Two carrots and two heads of celery will be sufficient.

Gravy Soup. No. 3.

Cut the lean part of a shin of beef, the same of a knuckle of veal, and set the bones of both on the fire, in two gallons of water, to make broth. Put the meat in a stewpan; add some lean bacon or ham, one carrot, two turnips, two heads of celery, two large onions, a bunch of sweet herbs, some whole pepper, two race of ginger, six cloves. Set these over the fire, let it draw till all the gravy is dried up to a nice brown; then add the broth that is made with the bones. Let it boil slowly four or five hours. Make the soup the day before you want to use it, that you may take the fat clean from the top, also the sediment from the bottom. Have ready some turnips, carrots, and cabbage lettuces, cut small, and one pint of young peas; add these to your soup; let it boil one hour, and it will be ready, with salt to your taste.

Hare Soup.

Skin the hare, and wash the inside well. Separate the limbs, legs, shoulders, and back; put them into a stewpan, with two glasses of port wine, an onion stuck with four cloves, a bundle of parsley, a little thyme, some sweet basil and marjoram, a pinch of salt, and cayenne pepper. Set the whole over a slow fire, and let it simmer for an hour; then add a quart of beef gravy and a quart of veal gravy; let the whole simmer gently till the hare is done. Strain the meat; then pass the soup through a sieve, and put a penny roll to soak in the broth. Take all the flesh of the hare from the bones, and pound it in a mortar, till fine enough to be rubbed through a sieve, taking care that none of the bread remains in it. Thicken the broth with the meat of the hare; rub it all together till perfectly fine, like melted butter, not thicker; heat it, and serve it up very hot. Be careful not to let it boil, as that will spoil it.

Another.

Half roast a good-sized hare; cut the back and legs in square pieces; stew the remaining part with five pints of good broth, a bunch of sweet herbs, three blades of mace, three large shalots, shred fine, two large onions, one head of celery, one dozen white pepper, eight cloves, and a slice of ham. Simmer the whole together three hours; then strain and rub it through a hair sieve with a wooden spoon; return the gravy into a stewpan; throw in the back and legs, and let it simmer three quarters of an hour before you send it to table.

Hessian Soup.

Take seven pints of water, one pint of split peas, one pound of lean beef, cut into small slices, three quarters of a pound of potatoes, three ounces of ground rice, two heads of celery, two onions, or leeks. Season with pepper and salt, and dried mint, according to your taste. Let it all boil slowly together till reduced to five pints.

Another.

One pound of beef, one pint of split peas, three turnips, four ounces ground rice, three potatoes, three onions, one head of celery, seven pints of water. Boil till reduced to six pints; then strain it through a hair sieve, with a little whole pepper.

Mock Turtle Soup. No. 1.

Take a calf's head, very white and very fresh, bone the nose part of it; put the head into some warm water to discharge the blood; squeeze the flesh with your hand to ascertain that it is all thoroughly out; blanch the head in boiling water. When firm, put it into cold water, which water must be prepared as follows: cut half a pound of fat bacon, a pound of beef suet, an onion stuck with two cloves, two thick slices of lemon; put these into a vessel, with water enough to contain the head; boil the head in this, and take it off when boiled, leaving it to cool. Then make your sauce in the following manner: put into a stewpan a pound of ham cut into slices; put over the ham two knuckles of veal, two large onions, and two carrots; moisten with some of the broth in which you have boiled the head to half the depth of the meat only; cover the stewpan, and set it on a slow fire to sweat through; let the broth reduce to a good rich colour; turn up the meat for fear of burning. When you have a very good colour, moisten with the whole remaining broth from the head; season with a very large bundle of sweet herbs, sweet basil, sweet marjoram, lemon-thyme, common thyme, two cloves, and a bay leaf, a few allspice, parsley, and green onions and mushrooms. Let the whole boil together for one hour; then drain it. Put into a stewpan a quarter of a pound of very fresh butter, let it melt over a very slow fire; put to this butter as much flour as it can receive till the flour has acquired a very good brown colour; moisten this gradually with the broth till you have employed it all; add half a bottle of good white wine; let the sauce boil that the flour may be well done; take off all the scum and fat; pass it through a sieve. Cut the meat off the calf's head in pieces of about an inch square; put them to boil in the sauce; season with salt, a little cayenne pepper, and lemon juice. Throw in some forcemeat balls, made according to direction, and a few hard yolks of eggs, and serve up hot.

Mock Turtle. No. 2.

Take a calf's head with the skin on; let it be perfectly well cleaned and scalded, if it is sent otherwise from the butcher's. You should examine and see that it is carefully done, and that it looks white and clean, by raising the skin from the bone with a knife. Boil it about twenty minutes; put it in cold

Mock Turtle. No. 3.

Neat's feet instead of calf's head; that is, two calf's feet and two neat's feet.

Mock Turtle. No. 4.

Two neat's and two calf's feet cut into pieces an inch long, and put into two quarts of strong mutton gravy, with a pint of Madeira. Take three dozen oysters, four anchovies, two onions, some lemon-peel, and mace, with a few sweet herbs; shred all very fine, with half a tea-spoonful of cayenne pepper, and add them to the feet. Let all stew together two hours and a quarter. Just before you send it to table, add the juice of two small lemons, and put forcemeat balls and hard eggs to it.

Mulligatawny Soup. No. 1.

Cut in pieces three fowls; reserve the best pieces of one of them for the terrine; cut the remainder very small: add to them a pound of lean ham, some garlic, bay-leaves, spices, whole mace, peppercorns, onions, pickles of any kind that are of a hot nature, and about four table-spoonfuls of good curry-powder. Cover the ingredients with four quarts of strong veal stock, and boil them till the soup is well flavoured: then strain that to the fowl you have reserved, which must be fried with onions. Simmer the whole till quite tender, and serve it up with plain boiled rice.

Mulligatawny Soup. No. 2.

Boil a knuckle of veal of about five pounds weight; let it stand till cold; then strain, and fry it in a little butter. Strain the liquor, and leave it till cold; take the fat off. Fry four onions brown in butter, add four dessert spoonfuls of curry-powder, a little turmeric, a little cayenne; put all these together in the soup. Let it simmer for two hours, and if not then thick enough, add a little suet and flour, and plain boiled rice to eat with it; and there should be a chicken or fowl, half roasted, and cut up in small pieces, then fried in butter of a light brown colour, and put into the soup instead of the veal, as that is generally too much boiled.

Mulligatawny Soup. No. 3.

Have some good broth made, chiefly of the knuckle of veal: when cold skim the fat off well, and pass the broth when in a liquid state through the sieve. Cut a chicken or rabbit into joints, (chicken or turkey is preferable to rabbit,) fry it well, with four or five middle-sized onions shred fine; shake a table-spoonful of curry-powder over it, and put it into the broth. Let it simmer three hours, and serve it up with a seasoning of cayenne pepper.

Onion Soup. No. 1.

Take twelve large Spanish onions, slice and fry them in good butter. Let them be done very brown, but not to burn, which they are apt to do when they are fried. Put to them two quarts of boiling water, or weak veal broth; pepper and salt to your taste. Let them stew till they are quite tender and almost dissolved; then add crumbs of bread made crisp, sufficient to make it of a proper thickness. Serve hot.

Onion Soup. No. 2.

Boil three pounds of veal with a handful of sweet herbs, and a little mace; when well boiled strain it through a sieve, skim off all the fat. Pare twenty-five onions; boil them soft, rub them through a sieve, and mix them with the veal gravy and a pint of cream, salt, and cayenne pepper, to your taste. Give it a boil and serve up; but do not put in the cream till it comes off the fire.

Onion Soup. No. 3.

Take two quarts of strong broth made of beef; twelve onions; cut these in four quarters, lay them in water an hour to soak. Brown four ounces of butter, put the onions into it, with some pepper and salt, cover them close, and let them stew till tender: cut a French loaf into slices, or sippets, and fry them in fresh butter; put them into your dish, and boil your onions and butter in your soup. When done enough, squeeze in the juice of a lemon, and pour it into your dish with the fried sippets. You may add poached eggs, if it pleases your palate.

Ox Head Soup.

Bone the head and cut it in pieces; wash it extremely clean from the blood; set it on the fire in three gallons of water. Put in a dozen onions, eight turnips, six anchovies, and a bundle of sweet herbs. Let all stew together very gently, till it is quite tender. Carefully skim off all the fat as it boils, but do not stir it. Take cabbage lettuce, celery, chervil, and turnips, all boiled tender and cut small; put them into the soup, and let them boil all together half an hour.

Another.

To half an ox's head put three gallons of water, and boil it three hours. Clean and cut it small and fine; let it stew for an hour with one pint of water, which must be put to it boiling; then add the three gallons boiling.

Green Pea Soup. No. 1.

Take a knuckle of veal of about four pounds, chop it in pieces, and set it on the fire in about six quarts of water, with a small piece of lean ham, three or four blades of mace, the same of cloves, about two dozen peppercorns, white and black, a small bundle of sweet herbs and parsley, and a crust of French roll toasted crisp. Cover close, and let it boil very gently over a slow fire till reduced to one half; then strain it off, and add a full pint of young green peas, a fine lettuce, cut small, four heads of celery, washed and cut small, about a quarter of a pound of fresh butter made hot, with a very little flour dredged into it, and some more lettuce cut small and thrown in. Just fry it a little; put it into the soup; cover it close, and let it stew gently over a slow fire two hours. Have a pint of old peas boiled in a pint of water till they are very tender, then pulp them through a sieve; add it to the soup, and let it all boil together, putting in a very little salt. There should be two quarts. Toast or fry some crust of French roll in dice.

Green Pea Soup. No. 2.

Put one quart of old green peas into a gallon of water, with a bunch of mint, a crust of bread, and two pounds of fresh meat of any sort. When these have boiled gently for three hours, strain the pulp through a colander; then fry spinach, lettuce, beet, and green onions, of each a handful, not too small, in butter, and one pint of green peas, boiled; pepper and salt. Mix all together, and let them just boil. The spinach must not be fried brown, but kept green.

Green Pea Soup. No. 3.

Boil the shells of your youngest peas in water till all the sweetness is extracted from them; then strain, and in that liquor boil your peas for the soup, with whole pepper and salt. When boiled, put them through a colander; have ready the young peas boiled by themselves; put a good piece of butter in a frying-pan with some flour, and into that some lettuce and spinach; fry it till it looks green, and put it into the soup with the young peas. When the greens are tender, it is done enough.

Green Pea Soup. No. 4.

Boil a quart of old peas in five quarts of water, with one onion, till they are soft; then work them through a sieve.—Put the pulp in the water in which the peas were boiled, with half a pint of young peas, and two cabbage lettuces, cut in slices; then let it boil half an hour; pepper and salt, to your taste.—Add a small piece of butter, mixed with flour, and one teaspoonful of loaf sugar.

Green Pea Soup. No. 5.

Make a good stock for your soup of beef, mutton, and veal; season to your palate; let it stand till cold, then take off all the fat. Take some old peas, boil them in water, with a sprig of mint and a large lettuce, strain them through a sieve; mix them with your soup till of proper thickness. Then add three quarters of a pint of cream; simmer it up together, and have ready half a pint of young peas, or asparagus, ready boiled to throw in. If the soup is not of a fine green, pound some spinach, and put in a little of the juice, but not too much.

Green Pea Soup. No. 6.

Take a quart of old peas, three or four cabbage lettuces, two heads of celery, two leeks, one carrot, two or three turnips, two or three old onions, and a little spinach that has been boiled; put them over the fire with some good consommé, and let them do gently, till all are very tender. Rub the whole through a tamis, or hair-sieve; put it in the pot. Have about half a pint of very young peas, and the hearts of two cabbage lettuces, cut fine and stewed down in a little broth. Put all together, with a small faggot of mint, and let it boil gently, skimming it well. When going to table, put into it fried bread, in dice, or crust of French roll. This quantity will be sufficient for a terrine.

Winter Pea Soup.

Take two quarts of old peas, a lettuce, a small bit of savoury, a handful of spinach, a little parsley, a cucumber, a bit of hock of bacon; stew all together till tender. Rub the whole through a colander; add to it some good gravy, and a little cayenne or common pepper. These quantities will be sufficient for a large terrine. Send it up hot with fried bread.

Pea Soup. No. 1.

Take two pints of peas, one pound of bacon, two bunches of carrots and onions, two bunches of parsley and thyme; moisten the whole with cold water, and let them boil for four hours, adding more water to them if necessary. When quite done, pound them in a mortar, and then rub them through a sieve with the liquor in which they have been boiling. Add a quart of the mixed jelly soup, boil it all together, and leave it on a corner of the fire till served. It must be thick and smooth as melted butter, and care taken throughout that it does not burn.

Pea Soup. No. 2.

Take about three or four pounds of lean beef; cut it in pieces and set it on the fire in three gallons of water, with nearly one pound of ham, a small bundle of sweet herbs, another of mint, and forty peppercorns. Wash a bunch of celery clean, put in the green tops; then add a quart of split peas. Cover it close, and let the whole boil gently till two parts out of three are wasted. Strain it off, and work it through a colander; put it into a clean saucepan with five or six heads of celery, washed and cut very small; cover it close, and let it stew till reduced to about three quarts: then cut some fat and lean bacon in dice, fry them just crisp; do the same by some bread, and put both into the soup. Season it with salt to your taste. When it is in the terrine, rub a little dried mint over it. If you chuse it, boil an ox's palate tender, cut it in dice, and put in, also forcemeat balls.

Pea Soup. No. 3.

To a quart of split peas put three quarts of water, two good turnips, one large head of celery, four onions, one blade of ginger, one spoonful of flour of mustard, and a small quantity of cayenne, black pepper, and salt. Let it boil over a slow fire till it is reduced to two quarts; then work it through a colander with a wooden spoon. Set it on the fire, and let it boil up; add a quarter of a pound of butter mixed with flour; beat up the yolks of three eggs, and stir it well in the soup. Gut a slice of bread into small dice; fry them of a light brown; put them into your soup-dish, and pour the soup over them.

Pea Soup. No. 4.

Boil one onion and one quart of peas in three quarts of water till they are soft; then work them through a hair sieve. Mix the pulp with the water in which the peas were boiled; set it over the fire and let it boil; add two cabbage lettuces, cut in slices, half a pint of young peas, and a little salt. Let it boil quickly half an hour; mix a little butter and flour, and boil in the soup.

Portable Soup.

Strip all the skin and fat off a leg of veal; then cut all the fleshy parts from the bone, and add a shin of beef, which treat in the same way; boil it slowly in three gallons of water or more according to the quantity of the meat; let the pot be closely covered: when you find it, in a spoon, very strong and clammy, like a rich jelly, take it off and strain it through a hair sieve into an earthen pan. After it is thoroughly cold, take off any fat that may remain, and divide your jelly clear of the bottom into small flatfish cakes in chinaware cups covered. Then place these cups in a large deep stewpan of boiling water over a stove fire, where let it boil gently till the jelly becomes a perfect glue; but take care the water does not get into the cups, for that will spoil it all. These cups of glue must be taken out, and, when cold, turn out the glue into a piece of new coarse flannel, and in about six hours turn it upon more fresh flannel, and keep doing this till it is perfectly dry—if you then lay it by in a dry warm place, it will presently become like a dry piece of glue. When you use it in travelling, take a piece the size of a large walnut, seasoning it with fresh herbs, and if you can have an old fowl, or a very little bit of fresh meat, it will be excellent.

Potato Soup.

Five large carrots, two turnips, three large mealy potatoes, seven onions, three heads of celery; slice them all thin, with a handful of sweet herbs; put them into one gallon of water, with bones of beef, or a piece of mutton; let them simmer gently till the vegetables will pulp through a sieve. Add cayenne pepper, salt, a pint of milk, or half a pint of cream, with a small piece of butter beaten up with flour.

Rabbit Soup.

One large rabbit, one pound of lean ham, one onion, one turnip, and some celery, two quarts of water; let them boil till the rabbit is tender. Strain off the liquor; boil a pint of cream, and add it to the best part of the rabbit pounded; if not of the thickness you wish, add some flour and butter, and rub it through a sieve. It must not be boiled after the cream is added.

Root Soup.

Potatoes, French turnips, English turnips, carrots, celery, of each six roots; pare and wash them; add three or four onions; set them on the fire with the bones of a rump of beef, or, if you have no such thing, about two pounds of beef, or any other beef bones. Chop them up, and put them on the fire with water enough to cover them; let them stew very gently till the roots are all tender enough to rub through a sieve. This done, cut a few roots of celery small, and put it to the strained soup. Season it with pepper and salt, and stew it gently till the celery is tender; then serve it with toast or fried bread. A bundle of herbs may be boiled in it, just to flavour it, and then taken out.

Scotch Leek Soup.

You make this soup to most advantage the day after a leg of mutton has been boiled, into the liquor from which put four large leeks, cut in pieces. Season with pepper and salt, and let it boil gently for a quarter of an hour. Mix half a pint of oatmeal with cold water till quite smooth; pour this into the soup; let it simmer gently half an hour longer; and serve it up.

To brown or colour Soup.

To brown soup, take two lumps of loaf-sugar in an iron spoon; let it stand on the stove till it is quite black, and put it into soup.

Seasoning for Soups and Brown Sauces.

Salt a bullock's liver, pressing it thoroughly with a great weight for four days. Take ginger and every sort of spice that is used to meat, and half a pound of brown sugar, a good quantity of saltpetre, and a pound of juniper-berries. Rub the whole in thoroughly, and let it lie six weeks in the liquor, boiling and skimming every three days, for an hour or two, till the liver becomes as hard as a board. Then steep it in the smoke liquor that is used for hams, and afterwards hang it up to smoke for a considerable time. When used, cut slices as thin as a wafer, and stew them down with the jelly of which you make your sauce or soup, and it will give a delightful flavour.

Soup. No. 1.

A quarter of a pound of portable soup, that is, one cake, in two quarts of boiling water; vegetables to be stewed separately, and added after the soup is dissolved.

Soup. No. 2.

Take a piece of beef about a stone weight, and a knuckle of veal, eight or ten onions, a bunch of thyme and parsley, an ounce of allspice, ten cloves, some whole pepper and salt; boil all these till the meat is all to pieces. Strain and take off the fat. Make about a quart of brown beef gravy with some of your broth; then take half a pound of butter and a good handful of flour mixed together, put it into a stewpan, set it over a slow fire, keeping it stirring till very brown; have ready what herbs you design for your soup, either endive or celery; chop them, but not too small; if you wish for a fine soup add a palate and sweetbreads, the palate boiled tender, and the sweetbreads fried, and both cut into small pieces. Put these, with herbs, into brown butter; put in as much of your broth as you intend for your soup, which must be according to the size of your dish. Give them a boil or two, then put in a quart of your gravy, and put all in a pot, with a fowl, or what you intend to put in your dish. Cover it close, and, let it boil an hour or more on a slow fire. Should it not be seasoned enough, add more salt, or what you think may be necessary: a fowl, or partridge, or squab pigeons, are best boiled in soup and to lie in the dish with it.

Soup. No. 3.

Cut three pounds of beef and one pound of veal in slices and beat it. Put half a pound of butter and a piece of bacon in your pan, brown it, and sprinkle in half a spoonful of flour. Cut two onions in; add pepper and salt, a bit of mace, and some herbs, then put in your meat, and fry it till it is brown on both sides. Have in readiness four quarts of boiling water, and a saucepan that will hold both water and what is in your frying-pan. Cover it close; set it over a slow fire and stew it down, till it is wasted to about five pints; then strain it off, and add to it what soup-herbs you like, according to your palate. Celery and endive must be first stewed in butter; and peas and asparagus first boiled, and well drained from the butter, before you put it to the soup. Stew it some time longer, and skim off all the fat; then take a French roll, which put in your soup-dish; pour in your soup, and serve it up. Just before you take it off the fire, squeeze in the juice of a lemon.

If veal alone is used, and fowl or chicken boiled in it and taken out when enough done, and the liquor strained, and the fowl or chicken put to the clear liquor, with vermicelli, you will have a fine white soup; and the addition of the juice of a lemon is a great improvement.

The French cooks put in chervil and French turnips, lettuce, sorrel, parsley, beets, a little bit of carrot, a little of parsnips, this last must not boil too long—all to be strained off: to be sent up with celery, endive (or peas) or asparagus, and stuffed cucumbers.

Soup without Meat.

Take two quarts of water, a little pepper, salt, and Jamaica pepper, a blade of mace, ten or twelve cloves, three or four onions, a crust of bread, and a bunch of sweet herbs; boil all these well. Take the white of two or three heads of endive, chopped, but not too small. Put three quarters of a pound of butter in a stewpan that will be large enough to hold all your liquor. Set it on a quick fire till it becomes very brown; then put a little of your liquor to prevent its turning, or oiling; shake in as much flour as will make it rather thick; then put in the endive and an onion shred small, stirring it well. Strain all your liquor, and put it to the butter and herbs; let it stew over a slow fire almost an hour. Dry a French roll, and let it remain in it till it is soaked through, and lay it in your dish with the soup. You may make this soup with asparagus, celery, or green peas, but they must be boiled before you put them to the burnt butter.

Soup for the Poor.

Eight pails of water, two quarts of barley, four quarts of split peas, one bushel of potatoes, half a bushel of turnips, half a bushel of carrots, half a peck of onions, one ounce of pepper, two pounds of salt, an ox's head, parsley, herbs, boiled six hours, produce one hundred and thirty pints. Boil the meat and take off the first scum before the other ingredients are put in.

Another.

To feed one hundred and thirty persons, take five quarts of Scotch barley, one quart of Scotch oatmeal, one bushel of potatoes, a bullock's head, onions, &c., one pound and half of salt.

Soup and Bouilli

may be made of ox-cheek, stewed gently for some hours, and well skimmed from the fat, and again when cold. Small suet dumplings are added when heated for table as soup.

Soupe à la Reine, or Queen's Soup.

Soak a knuckle of veal and part of a neck of mutton in water; put them in a pot with liquor, carrots, turnips, thyme, parsley, and onions. Boil and scum it; then season with a head or two of celery; boil this down; take half a pound of blanched almonds, and beat them; take two fowls, half roasted, two sweetbreads set off; beat these in a mortar, put them in your stock, with the crumbs of two French rolls; then rub them through a tamis and serve up.

Another.

For a small terrine take about three quarters of a pound of almonds; blanch, and pound them very fine. Cut up a fowl, leaving the breast whole, and stew in consommé. When the breast is tender, take it out, (leaving the other parts to stew with the consommé) pound it well with the almonds and three hard-boiled yolks of eggs, and take it out of the mortar. Strain the consommé, and put it, when the fat is skimmed off, to the almonds, &c. Have about a quarter of a pint of Scotch barley boiled very tender, add it to the other ingredients, put them into a pot with the consommé, and stir it over the fire till it is boiling hot and well mixed. Rub it through a tamis, and season it with a little salt; it must not boil after being rubbed through.

Soupe Maigre. No. 1.

Take the white part of eight loaved lettuces, cut them as small as dice, wash them and strain them through a sieve. Pick a handful of purslain and half a handful of parsley, wash and drain them. Cut up six large cucumbers in slices about the thickness of a crown-piece. Peel and mince four large onions, and have in readiness three pints of young green peas. Put half a pound of fresh butter into your stewpan; brown it of a high colour, something like that of beef gravy. Put in two ounces of lean bacon cut clean from the rind, add all your herbs, peas, and cucumbers, and thirty corns of whole pepper; let these stew together for ten minutes; keep stirring to prevent burning. Put one gallon of boiling water to a gallon of small broth, and a French roll cut into four pieces toasted of a fine yellow brown. Cover your stewpan, and let it again stew for two hours. Add half a drachm of beaten mace, one clove beaten, and half a grated nutmeg, and salt to your taste. Let it boil up, and squeeze in the juice of a lemon. Send it to table with all the bread and the herbs that were stewed in it.

Soupe Maigre. No. 2.

Take of every vegetable you can get, excepting cabbage, in such quantity as not to allow any one to predominate; cut them small and fry them brown in butter; add a little water, and thicken with flour and butter. Let this stew three hours very gently; and season to your taste. The French add French rolls.

Soupe Maigre. No. 3.

Half a pound of butter, put in a stewpan over the fire, and let it brown. Cut two or three onions in slices, two or three heads of celery, two handfuls of spinach, a cabbage, two turnips, a little parsley, three cabbage lettuces, a little spice, pepper and salt. Stew all these about half an hour; then add about two quarts of water, and let it simmer till all the roots are tender. Put in the crust of a French roll, and send it to table.

Soupe Maigre. No. 4.

Cut three carrots, three turnips, three heads of celery, three leeks, six onions, and two cabbage lettuces in small pieces; put them in your stewpan with a piece of butter, the size of an egg, a pint of dried or green peas, and two quarts of water, with a little pepper and salt. Simmer the whole over the fire till tender; then rub it through a sieve or tamis; add some rice, and let it simmer an hour before you serve it up.

Soupe Maigre. No. 5.

Take three carrots, three turnips, three heads of celery, three leeks, six onions, two cabbage lettuces; cut them all in small pieces, and put them in your stewpan, with a piece of butter about the size of an egg, and a pint of dried or green peas, and two quarts of water. Simmer them over the fire till tender, then rub through a sieve or tamis. Add some rice, and let it simmer an hour before you serve it up.

Soupe Santé, or Wholesome Soup.

Take beef and veal cut in thin slices; put sliced turnips, carrots, onions, bacon, in the bottom of your stewpan; lay your meat upon these, and over it some thin thyme, parsley, a head or two of celery. Cover the whole down; set it over a charcoal fire; draw it down till it sticks to the bottom; then fill up with the above stock. Let it boil slowly till the goodness is extracted from your meat; then strain it off. Cut and wash some celery, endive, sorrel, a little chervil, spinach, and a piece of leek; put these in a stewpan, with a bit of butter. Stew till tender, then put this in your soup; give it a boil up together, and skim the fat off. Cut off the crust of French rolls; dry and soak them in some of your soup; put them into it, and serve your soup.

Spanish Soup.

Put the scrag end of a neck of veal, two calves' feet, two pounds of fresh beef, one old fowl, into a pot well tinned, with six quarts of water, and a little salt, to raise the scum, which must be very carefully taken off. Let these boil very gently two hours and a half, till the water is reduced to four quarts; then take out all the meat, strain the broth, and put to it a small quantity of pepper, mace, cloves, and cinnamon, finely pounded, with four or five cloves of garlic. A quarter of an hour afterwards add eight or ten ounces of rice, with six ounces of ham or bacon, and a drachm of saffron put into a muslin bag. Observe to keep it often stirred after the rice is in, till served up. It will be ready an hour and a half after the saffron is in. You should put a fowl into it an hour before it is ready, and serve it up whole in the soup.

This soup will keep two or three days.

Turnip Soup.

Make a good strong gravy of beef or mutton; let it stand till cold; take off all the fat; pare some turnips and slice them thin; stew them till tender, then strain them through a sieve; mix the pulp with the gravy, till of a proper thickness:—then add three quarters of a pint of cream; boil it up, and send it to table.

Veal Soup.

Take a knuckle of veal, and chop it into small pieces; set it on the fire with four quarts of water, pepper, mace, a few herbs, and one large onion. Stew it five or six hours; then strain off the spice, and put in a pint of green peas until tender. Take out the small bones, and send the rest up with the soup.

Vegetable Soup. No. 1.

Take a quart of beef jelly and the same quantity of veal jelly: boil it, have some carrots and turnips, cut small, previously boiled in a little of the jelly; throw them in, and serve it up hot.

Vegetable Soup. No. 2.

Take two cabbage and two coss lettuces, one hard cabbage, six onions, one large carrot, two turnips, three heads of celery, a little tarragon, chervil, parsley, and thyme, chopped fine, and a little flour fried in a quarter of a pound of butter (or less will do). Then add three quarts of boiling water;

boil it for two hours, stir it well, and add, before sending it to table, some crumbs of stale bread: the upper part of the loaf is best.

Vegetable Soup. No. 3.

Let a quantity of dried peas (split peas), or haricots, (lentils) be boiled in common water till they are quite tender; let them then be gradually passed through a sieve with distilled water, working the mixture with a wooden spoon, to make what the French call a *puré*: and let it be made sufficiently liquid with distilled water to bear boiling down. Then let a good quantity of fresh vegetables, of any or all kinds in their season, especially carrots, lettuces, turnips, celery, spinach, with always a few onions, be cut into fine shreds, and put it into common boiling water for three or four minutes to blanch; let them then be taken out with a strainer, added to and mixed with the *puré*, and the whole set to boil gently at the fire for at least two hours. A few minutes before taking the soup from the fire, let it be seasoned to the taste with pepper and salt.

The soup, when boiling gently at the fire, should be very frequently stirred, to prevent its sticking to the side of the pan, and acquiring a burnt taste.

Vegetable Soup. No. 4.

Cut two potatoes, one turnip, two heads of celery, two onions, one carrot, a bunch of sweet herbs; put them all into a stewpan; cover close; draw them gently for twenty minutes, then put two quarts of good broth, let it boil gently, and afterwards simmer for two hours. Strain through a fine sieve; put it into your pan again; season with pepper and salt, and let it boil up.

Vegetable Soup. No. 5.

Take four turnips, two potatoes, three onions, three heads of celery, two carrots, four cabbage lettuces, a bunch of sweet herbs, and parsley. The vegetables must be cut in slices; put them into a stewpan, with half a pint of water; cover them close; set them over the fire for twenty minutes to draw; add three pints of broth or water, and let it boil quickly. When the vegetables are tender rub them through a sieve. If you make the soup with water, add butter, flour, pepper, and salt. Let it be of the thickness of good cream, and add some fine crumbs of bread with small dumplings.

Vermicelli Soup.

Break the vermicelli a little, throw it into boiling water, and let it boil about two minutes. Strain it in a sieve, and throw it into cold water: then strain and put it into a good clear consommé, and let it boil very slowly about a quarter of an hour. When it is going to table, season with a little salt, and put into it a little crust of French roll.

West India Soup, called Pepper Pot.

A small knuckle of veal and a piece of beef of about three pounds, seven or eight pounds of meat in all; potherbs as for any other soup. When the soup is skimmed and made, strain it off. The first ingredient you add to the soup must be some dried ocre (a West India vegetable), the quantity according to your judgment. It is hard and dry, and therefore requires a great deal of soaking and boiling. Then put in the spawn of the lobsters you intend for your soup, first pounding it very fine, and mixing it by degrees with a little of your soup cooled, or it will be lumpy, and not so smooth as it should be. Put it into the soup-pot, and continue to stir some time after it is in. Take about two middling handfuls of spinach and about six hearts of the inside of very nice greens; scald both greens and spinach before you put them to the soup, to take off the rawness; the greens require most scalding. Squeeze them quite dry, chop and put them into the soup; then add all the fat and inside egg and spawn you can get from the lobsters, also the meat out of the tails and claws. Add the green tops only of a large bundle of asparagus, of the sort which they call sprew-grass, previously scalded; a few green peas also are very good. After these ingredients are in, the soup should no more than simmer; and when the herbs are sufficiently tender it is done enough. This soup is not to be clear, on the contrary thick with the lobster, and a perfect mash with the lobster and greens. You are to put in lobster to your liking; I generally put in five or six, at least of that part of them which is called fat, egg, and inside spawn, sufficient to make it rich and good. It should look quite yellow with this. Put plenty of the white part also, and in order that none of the goodness of the lobsters should be lost, take the shells of those which you have used, bruise them in a mortar, and boil them in some of the broth, to extract what goodness remains; then strain off the liquor and add it to the rest. Scoop some potatoes round, half boiling them first, and put into it. Season with red pepper. Put in a piece of nice pickled pork, which must be first scalded, for fear of its being too salt; stew it with the rest and serve it.

White Soup. No. 1.

Take two chickens; skin them; take out the lungs and wash them thoroughly; put them in a stewpan with some parsley. Add a quart of veal jelly, and stew them in this for one hour over a very slow fire. Then take out the chickens, and put a penny roll to soak in the liquor; take all the flesh of the chickens from the bones, and pound it in a mortar, with the yolk of three eggs boiled hard. Add the bread (when soaked enough) and pound it also with them; then rub the whole finely through a sieve. Add a quart more jelly to the soup, and strain it through a sieve; then put the chicken to the soup. Set a quart of cream on the fire till it boils, stirring it all the time; when ready to serve, pour that into the soup and mix it well together. Have ready a little vermicelli, boiled in a little weak broth, to throw into the soup, when put into the terrine.

White Soup. No. 2.

Have good stock made of veal and beef; then take about a pound of veal, and the like quantity of ham, cut both into thin slices, and put them into a stewpan, with a pint of water and two onions cut small. Set it on the fire and stew it down gently, till it is quite dry, and of a rather light brown colour; then add the stock, and let it all stew till the veal and ham are quite tender. Strain it off into the stewpot; add a gill or more of cream, some blanched rice boiled tender, the quantity to your own judgment, the yolks of six eggs beaten up well with a little new milk: let the soup be boiling hot before the eggs are added, which put to it by degrees, keeping it stirring over a slow fire. Serve it very hot: to prevent curdling, put the soup-pot into a large pot of boiling water, taking care that not the least drop of water gets in, and so make it boiling hot.

White Soup. No. 3.

Cut one pound of veal, or half a fowl, into small pieces; put to it a few sweet herbs, a crust of bread, an ounce of pearl barley well washed. Set it over a slow fire, closely covered; let it boil till half is consumed; then strain it and take off the fat. Have ready an ounce of sweet almonds blanched, pound them in a marble mortar, adding a little soup to prevent their oiling. Mix all together. When you send it up, add one third of new milk or cream, salt and pepper to taste.

White Soup. No. 4.

Take a knuckle of veal, and put water according to the quantity of soup you require; let it boil up and skim it; then put in three ounces of lean bacon or ham, with two heads of celery, one carrot, one turnip, two onions, and three or four blades of mace, and boil for three or four hours. When properly boiled, strain it off, taking care to skim off all the fat; then put into it two ounces of rice, well boiled, half a pint of cream beaten up, and five or six yolks of eggs. When ready to serve, pour the soup to the eggs backward and forward to prevent it from curdling, and send it to table. You must boil the soup once after you add the cream, and before you put it to the eggs. Three laurel leaves put into it in summer and six in winter make a pleasant addition, instead of sweet almonds.

White Soup. No. 5.

Make your stock with veal and chicken, and beat half a pound of almonds in a mortar very fine, with the breast of a fowl. Put in some white broth, and strain off. Stove it gently, and poach eight eggs, and lay in your soup, with a French roll in the middle, filled with minced chicken or veal, and serve very hot.

White Soup. No. 6.

Take a knuckle of veal; stew it with celery, herbs, slices of ham, and a little cayenne and white pepper; season it to your taste. When it is cleared off, add one pound of sweet almonds, a pint of cream, and the yolks of eight eggs, boiled hard and finely bruised. Mix these all together in your soup; let it just boil, and send it up hot. You may add a French roll; let it be nicely browned.

The ingredients here mentioned will make four quarts.

White Soup. No. 7.

Stock from a boiled knuckle of veal, thickened with about two ounces of sweet almonds, beaten to a paste, with a spoonful of water to prevent their oiling; a large slice of dressed veal, and a piece of crumb of bread, soaked in good milk, pounded and rubbed through a sieve; a bit of fresh lemon-peel and a blade of mace in the finest powder. Boil all together about half an hour, and stir in about a pint of cream without boiling.

BROTHS.

Broth for the Poor.

A good wholesome broth may be made at a very reasonable rate to feed the poor in the country. The following quantities would furnish a good meal for upwards of fifty persons.

Take twenty pounds of the very coarse parts of beef, five pounds of whole rice, thirteen gallons of water; boil the meat in the water first, and skim it very well; then put in the rice, some turnips, carrots, leeks, celery, thyme, parsley, and a good quantity of potatoes; add a good handful of salt, and boil them all together till tender.

Another.

Four hundred quarts of good broth for the poor may be made as follows: —Good beef, fifty pounds weight; beeves' cheeks, and legs of beef, five; rice, thirty pounds; peas, twenty-three quarts; black pepper, five ounces and a half; cayenne pepper, half an ounce; ground ginger, two ounces; onions, thirteen pounds; salt, seven pounds and a half; with celery, leeks, carrots, dried mint, and any other vegetable.

Broth for the Sick. No. 1.

Boil one ounce of very lean veal, fifteen minutes in a little butter, and then add half a pint of water; set it over a very slow fire, with a spoonful of barley and a piece of gum arabic about the size of a nut.

Broth for the Sick. No. 2.

Put a leg of beef and a scrag of mutton cut in pieces into three or four gallons of water, and let them boil twelve hours, occasionally stirring them well; and cover close. Strain the broth, and let it stand till it will form a jelly; then take the fat from the top and the dross from the bottom.

Broth for the sick. No. 3.

Take twelve quarts of water, two knuckles of veal, a leg of beef, or two shins, four calves' feet, a chicken, a rabbit, two onions, cloves, pepper, salt, a bunch of sweet herbs. Cover close, and let the whole boil till reduced to six quarts. Strain and keep it for use.

Barley Broth.

Take four or five pounds of the lean end of a neck of mutton, soak it well in cold water for some time, then put it in a saucepan with about four quarts of water and a tea-cupful of fine barley. Just before it boils take it off the fire and skim it extremely well; put in salt and pepper to your taste, and a small bundle of sweet herbs, which take out before the broth is sent up. Then let it boil very gently for some hours afterwards; add turnips, carrots, and onions, cut in small pieces, and continue to boil the broth till the vegetables are quite done and very tender. When nearly done it requires to be stirred frequently lest the barley should adhere.

Another.

Put on whatever bones you have; stew them down well with a little whole pepper, onions, and herbs. When done, strain it off, and next day take off all the fat. Take a little pearl barley, boil it a little and strain it off; put it to the broth, add a coss lettuce, carrot, and turnip, cut small. Boil all together some time, and serve it up.

Chervil Broth for Cough.

Boil a calf's liver and two large handfuls of chervil in four quarts of spring water till reduced to one quart. Strain it, and take a coffee-cupful night and morning.

Hodge-Podge.

Stew a scrag of mutton: put in a peck of peas, a bunch of turnips cut small, a few carrots, onions, lettuce, and some parsley. When sufficiently boiled add a few mutton chops, which must stew gently till done.

Leek Porridge.

Peel twelve leeks; boil them in water till tender; take them out and put them into a quart of new milk; boil them well; thicken up with oatmeal, and add salt according to the taste.

Madame de Maillet's Broth.

Two ounces of veal, six carrots, two turnips, one table-spoonful of gum arabic, one table-spoonful of rice, two quarts of water; simmer for about two hours.

Mutton Broth.

The bone of a leg of mutton to be chopped small, and put into the stewpan with vegetables and herbs, together with a little drop of water, and drawn as gravy soup; add boiling water.

Pork Broth.

Take a leg of pork fresh cut up; beat it and break the bone; put it into three gallons of soft water, with half an ounce of mace and the same quantity of nutmeg. Let it boil very gently over a slow fire, until two thirds of the water are consumed. Strain the broth through a fine sieve, and when it is cold take off the fat. Drink a large cupful in the morning fasting, and between meals, and just before going to bed, warmed. Season it with a little salt. This is a fine restorative.

Potage.

Boil a leg of beef, and a knuckle of veal, with a bunch of sweet herbs, a little mace and whole pepper, and a handful of salt. When the meat is boiled to rags or to a very strong broth, strain it through a hair sieve, and when it is cold, take off the fat. With raw beef make a gravy thus: cut your beef in pieces, put them in a frying-pan with a piece of butter or a slice of bacon, fry it very brown, then put it to some of your strong broth, and when it grows browner and thick till it becomes reduced to three pints of gravy, fill up your strong broth to boil with a piece of butter and a handful of sweet herbs. Afterwards a chicken must be boiled and blanched and cut in slices; and two or three sweetbreads fried very brown; a turnip also sliced and fried. Boil all these half an hour, and put them in the dish in which you intend to serve up, with three French rolls (cut in halves) and set it over a fire with a quart of your gravy, and some of your broth, covered with a dish, till it boils very fast, and as it reduces fill up with your broth till your bread is quite soaked. You may put into the dish either a duck, pigeon, or any bird you please; but whichever you choose, roast it first, and then let it boil in the dish with your bread. This may be made a pea soup, by only rubbing peas through a sieve.

Scotch Pottage.

Place a tin saucepan on the fire with some boiling water; stir in Scotch oatmeal till it is of the desired consistency: when done, pour it in a basin and add milk or cream to it. It is more nutritious to make it of milk instead of water, if the stomach will bear it. The Scotch peasantry live entirely on this strengthening food. The best Scotch oatmeal is to be bought at Dudgeon's, in the Strand.

Scotch Broth.

Boil very tender a piece of thin brisket of beef, with trimmings of any other meat, or a piece of gravy beef; cut it into square pieces; strain off the broth and put it in a soup-pot; add the beef, cut in squares, with plenty of carrots, turnips, celery, and onions, cut in shapes and well boiled before put to the broth, and, if liked, some very small suet dumplings first boiled. Season it to your palate.

Turnip Broth.

Have a sufficient quantity of good strong broth as for any other soup, taking care that it is not too strongly flavoured by any of the roots introduced into it. Peel a good quantity of the best turnips, selecting such as are not bitter. Sweat them in butter and a little water till they are quite tender. Rub them through a tamis, mix them with the broth; boil it for about half an hour. Add half a pint of very good cream, and be careful not to have too fierce a fire, as it is apt to burn.

Another.

Put one pound of lean veal, pulled into small pieces in a pipkin, with two large or three middling turnips. Cover the pipkin very close, to prevent water from getting into it; set it in a pot of water, and let it boil for two or three hours. A tea-cupful of the broth produced in the pipkin may be taken twice or thrice a day.

Veal Broth. No. 1.

Take ten or twelve knuckles, such as are cut off from legs and shoulders of mutton, at the very shank; rub them with a little salt, put them in a pan of water for two or three hours, and wash them very clean; boil them in a gallon of spring water for an hour. Strain them very clean, then put in two ounces of hartshorn shavings, and the bottom crust of a penny loaf; let it boil till the water is reduced to about three pints; strain it off, and when cold skim off the fat. Take half a pint warm before you rise, and the same in bed at night. Make it fresh three times a week in summer, and twice a week in winter: do not put in any lamb bones. This is an excellent thing.

Veal Broth. No. 2.

Soak a knuckle of veal for an hour in cold water; put it into fresh water over the fire, and, as the scum rises, take it off; let it stew gently for two hours, with a little salt to make the scum rise. When it is sufficiently stewed, strain the broth from the meat. Put in some vermicelli; keep the meat hot; and as you are going to put the soup into the terrine add half a pint of cream.

Veal Broth. No. 3.

Take one pound of lean veal, one blade of mace, two table-spoonfuls of rice, one quart of water; let it boil slowly two hours; add a little salt.

Veal Broth. No. 4.—Excellent for a Consumption.

Boil a knuckle of veal in a gallon of water; skim and put to it half a pound of raisins of the sun, stoned, and the bottoms of two manchets, with a nutmeg and a half sliced, and a little hartshorn. Let it boil till reduced to half the quantity; then pound it all together and strain. Add some brown sugar-candy, some rose-water, and also the juice of a lemon, if the patient has no cough.

FISH.

Carp and Tench.

SCALE the fish, take out the gut and gall; save all the blood. Split the carp if large; cut it in large pieces, and salt it. Boil some sliced parsley roots and onions tender in half a pint of water, adding a little cayenne pepper, ginger, cloves, and allspice, a lemon sliced, a little vinegar, and moist sugar, one glass of red wine, and some butter rolled in flour. Then put in the fish, and let it boil very fast for half an hour in a stewpan. The blood is to be put in the sauce.

Carp, to stew.

Scale, gut, and cleanse them; save the roes and milts; stew them in some good broth: season, to your taste, with a bundle of herbs, onions, anchovies, and white wine; and, when they are stewed enough, thicken the sauce with the yolks of five eggs. Pass off the roes, dip them in yolk of egg and flour, and fry them with some sippets of French bread; then fry a little parsley, and, when you serve up, garnish the dish with the roes, parsley, and sippets.

Another way.

Have your carp fresh out of the water; scale and gut them, washing the blood out of each fish with a little claret; and save that after so doing. Cut your carp in pieces, and stew in a little fresh butter, a few blades of mace, winter savory, a little thyme, and three or four onions; after stewing awhile, take them out, put them by, and fold them up in linen, till the liquor is ready to receive them again, as the fish would otherwise be boiled to pieces before the liquor was reduced to a proper thickness. When you have taken out your fish, put in the claret that you washed out the blood with, and a pint of beef or mutton gravy, according to the quantity of your fish, with some salt and the butter in which you stewed the carp; and when this butter is almost boiled to a proper thickness put in your fish again; stew all together, and serve it up. Two spoonfuls of elder vinegar to the liquor when taken up will give a very agreeable taste.

Cod, to stew.

Cut a cod into thin pieces or slices; lay them in rows at the bottom of a dish; put in a pint of white wine, half a pound of butter, a few oysters, with their liquor, a little pepper and salt, with some crumbs of bread. Stew them all till they are done enough. Garnish the dish with lemon.

Cod, Ragout of.

Wash the cod clean, and boil it in warm water, with vinegar, pepper, salt, a bay-leaf, and lemon. Make a sauce of burnt butter, fried flour, capers, and oysters. When you serve it up put in some black pepper and lemon-juice.

Cod's Head, to boil.

Take vinegar and salt, a bunch of sweet herbs, and an onion; set them on the fire in a kettle of water; boil them and put in the head; and, while it is boiling, put in cold water and vinegar. When boiled, take it up, put it into a dish, and make sauce as follows:—Take gravy and claret, boiled with a bundle of sweet herbs and an onion, two or three anchovies, drawn with two pounds of butter, a pint of shrimps, oysters, the meat of a lobster shred fine. You may stick little toasts on the head, and lay on and about the roe, milt, and liver. Garnish the dish with fried parsley, lemon, barberries, horseradish, and fried fish.

Crab, to dress.

Take all the body and the meat of the legs, and put them together in a dish to heat, with a little broth or gravy, just to make them moist. When hot, have ready some good broth or gravy, with an anchovy dissolved in it, and the juice of a small lemon, heated; afterwards thicken it up with butter, and stir it in the crab, as it is, hot: then serve all up in the shell.

Crab or Lobster, to butter.

The crabs or lobsters being boiled and cold, take all the meat out of the shells and body; break the claws and take out the meat. Shred it small; add a spoonful or two of claret, a little vinegar, and a grated nutmeg. Let it boil up till it is thoroughly hot; then put in some melted butter, with anchovies and white gravy; thicken with the yolk of an egg or two, and when very hot put it into the large shell. Put crumbs of bread over it, and brown it with a salamander.

Crab, or Lobster, to stew. No. 1.

A little cayenne, vinegar, butter, flour, and salt. Cover it with water and let it stew gently.

Crab, or Lobster, to stew. No. 2.

When the lobsters are boiled, take out the tail and claws, and dip them in white wine; strew over them nutmeg, cloves, mace, salt, and pepper, mixed together. Then pour over them some melted butter with a little white wine in it; send them to the bakehouse, and let them stand in a slow oven about half an hour. Pour out the butter and wine, and pour on some fresh butter; when cold, cover them, and keep them in a cold place.

Crab, or Lobster, to stew. No. 3.

Boil the lobsters; when cold take out all the meat; season it well with pepper, salt, nutmeg and mace pounded. Put it into an earthen pot with as much clarified butter as will cover it; bake it well. While warm, take it out of the pot, and let the butter drain from it. Break it as fine as you can with a spoon or knife; add more seasoning if required; put it as close as possible in the pot, and cover with clarified butter. The hen lobsters are best for this purpose, as the eggs impart a good colour. It may be pounded in a marble mortar, but, if baked enough, will do as well without it.

Crawfish, to make red.

Rub the fish with aqua vitæ, which will produce the desired effect most completely.

Eels broiled whole.

Skin, wash, and dry your eels, and score them with the knife, seasoning them with pepper, salt, thyme, parsley, and crumbs of bread, turning them round and skewering them across; you may either roast or broil them as you like best: the sauce to be melted butter with lemon juice.

Eels, to collar.

Scour large silver eels with salt; slit them, and take out the back-bones; wash and dry them; season with shred parsley, sage, an onion, and thyme. Then roll each into collars, in a cloth; tie them close with the heads, bones, and a bundle of herbs, and boil them in salt and water. When tender, take them up, and again tie them close; drain the pickle, and put them into it.

Eels, to fry.

Cut every eel into eight pieces; mix them with a proper quantity of yolks of eggs, and well season with pepper, and salt, and bread rubbed fine, with parsley and thyme; then flour them, and fry them. You may cook them as plain as you like, with only salt and flour, and serve them up with melted butter and fried parsley.

Eels, to pot.

Into an earthen pan put Jamaica and common pepper, pounded fine, and salt; mix them and strew some at the bottom of the pan; cut your eels and lay them over it, and strew a little more seasoning over them. Then put in another layer of eels, repeating this process till all the eels are in. Lay a few bay leaves upon them, and pour as much vinegar as you may think requisite; cover the pan with brown paper and bake them. Pour off the liquor, cover them with clarified butter, and lay them by for use.

Eels, to pickle.

Drain, wash, and well cleanse your eels, and cut off the heads. Cut them in lengths of four or five inches, with their skins on; stew in them some pepper and salt, and broil them on a gridiron a fine colour: then put them in layers in a jar, with bay-leaf, pepper, salt, a few slices of lemon, and a few cloves. Pour some good vinegar on them; tie strong paper over, and prick a few holes in it. It is better to boil the seasoning with some sweet herbs in the vinegar, and let it stand to be cold before it is put over the eels. Two yolks of eggs boiled hard should be put in the vinegar with a tea-spoonful of flour of mustard. Two yolks are sufficient for twelve pounds of eels.

Eels, to roast.

Skin your eels; turn, scotch, and wash them with melted butter; skewer them crosswise; fix them on the spit, and put over them a little pepper, salt, parsley, and thyme; roast them quick. Fry some parsley, and lay it round the dish; make your sauce of butter and gravy.

Eels, to spitchcock.

Leave the skin on the eels; scour them with salt; wash them; cut off their heads and slit them on the belly side; take out the bone and guts. Wash and wipe them well; cut them in pieces three inches long, and wipe them quite dry. Put two ounces of butter, with a little minced parsley, thyme, sage, pepper and salt, and a little chopped shalot, in a stewpan; when the butter is melted, stir the ingredients together, and take the pan off the fire; mix the yolks of two eggs with them and dip the eels in, a piece at a time; then roll them in bread crumbs, making as much stick on as you can. Rub the gridiron with a bit of suet; set it over a clear fire, and broil your eels of a fine crisp brown; dust them with crisp parsley. Sauce, anchovy and butter, or plain butter in a boat.

Another way.

Wash your eels well in their skins with salt and water; dry and slit them; take out the back-bone, and slash them: season them with chopped parsley, thyme, salt, and pepper. Clean the inside with melted butter; cut them into pieces about three inches long and broil them; make the sauce with butter and orange juice.

Eels, to stew.

Take five pounds of middling shafflings, cut off their heads, skin, and cut them in pieces as long as your finger. Wash them in several waters; dry them well with a cloth, lay them in a pan, sprinkle over them half an ounce of white salt, and let them lie an hour. Lay them in a stewpan, and add half a pint of French white wine, a quarter of a pint of water, two cloves beaten, a blade of mace, a large onion peeled, and the rind of a lemon; stew all these gently half an hour: then take the eels out of the liquor, skim off all the fat, and flour the eels all over; put to the liquor in which they were stewed an anchovy, washed and boned, and mix sorrel and parsley, half a handful of each, and half a pound of fresh butter. Let it just boil up; put in the eels; when they boil, lay them on sippets in your dish, and send them up hot to table.

Another way.

Cover the fish close in a stewpan with a piece of butter as big as a walnut rolled in flour, and let it stew till done enough, which you will know by the eels being very tender. Take them up and lay them on a dish; strain your sauce, and give it a quick boil and pour it over the fish. Garnish with lemon.

Fish, to recover when tainted.

When fish of any kind is tainted plunge it in cold milk, which will render it sweet again.

Fish, in general, to dress.

Take water, salt, half a pint of vinegar, a sprig of thyme, a small onion, and a little lemon peel; boil them all together, then put in your fish, and when done enough take them out, drain them well, and lay them over a stove to keep hot.

If you fry fish, strew some crumbs of grated bread very fine over them, and fry them in sweet oil; then drain them well and keep them hot.

Fish, to dress in Sauce.

Cut off the heads, tails, and fins, of two or three haddocks or other small fish; stew them in a quart of water, with a little spice and anchovy, and a bunch of sweet herbs, for a quarter of an hour; and then skim. Roll a bit of butter in flour, and thicken the liquor; put down the fish, and stew them with a little chopped parsley, and cloves, or onions.

Fish hashed in Paste.

Cut the fish into dice about three quarters of an inch square; prepare white sauce the same as for fowls, leaving out the mushrooms and truffles; add a little anchovy sauce to give it a good colour, and a pinch of cayenne pepper and salt. When the sauce is done, throw in the dice of fish, and when thoroughly hot serve it.

There should be a little more butter in the sauce than is commonly used in the white sauce for fowls.

Fish, to Cavietch.

Cut the fish into slices, season them with pepper and salt, and let them lie for an hour; dry them well with a cloth, flour and fry them brown in oil: boil a quantity of vinegar proportionate to that of the fish to be prepared: cover the fish with slices of garlic and some whole pepper and mace; add the same quantity of oil as vinegar, mix them well together, and salt to your taste. When the fish and liquor are quite cold, slice onions and lay at the bottom of the pan; then put a layer of fish, and so on, till the whole is in. The liquor must be cold before it is poured on the fish.

Gudgeon.

Dress as you would smelts.

Haddocks, to bake.

Bone two or three haddocks, and lay them in a deep pan with pepper, salt, butter and flour, and two or three anchovies, and sufficient water to cover them. Cover the pan close for an hour, which is required to bake them, and serve them in the saucepan.

Haddock baked.

Let the inside of the gills be drawn out and washed clean; fill with bread crumbs, parsley, sweet herbs chopped, nutmeg, salt, pepper, a bit of butter, and grated lemon-peel; skewer the tail into the mouth, and rub it well with yolk of egg. Strew over bread crumbs, and stick on bits of butter. Bake the fish in a common oven, putting into the dish a little white wine and water, a bit of mace, and lemon-peel. Serve up with oyster sauce, white fish sauce, or anchovy sauce; but put to the sauce what gravy is in the dish, first skimming it.

Haddock Pudding.

Skin the fish; take out all the bones, and cut it in thin slices. Butter the mould well, and throw round it the spawn of a lobster, before it is boiled. Put alternate slices of haddock and lobster in the mould, and season to your taste. Beat up half a pint of cream or more, according to the size of the mould, with three eggs, and pour on it: tie a cloth over, and boil it an hour. Stew oysters to go in the dish. Garnish with pastry.

Herring.

The following is a Swedish dish: Take salted herring, some cold veal, an apple, and an onion, mince them all fine, and mix them well together with oil and vinegar.

Lampreys, to pot.

Well cleanse your lampreys in the following manner: the intestines and the pipe which nature has given them instead of a bone must be taken clear away, by opening them down the belly from head to tail. They must then be rubbed with wood-ashes, to remove the slime. Then rub with salt, and wash them in three or four waters. Let them be quite free from water before you proceed to season them thus:—take, according to the quantity you intend to pot, allspice ground with an equal quantity of black pepper, a little mace, cayenne pepper, salt, about the same quantity as that of all the other seasoning; mix these well together, and rub your lampreys inside and out. Put them into an earthen pan or a well-tinned copper stewpan, with some good butter under and over, sufficient to cover them, when dissolved. Put in with them a few bay-leaves and the peel of a lemon. Let them bake slowly till they are quite done; then strain off the butter, and let them lie on the back of a sieve till nearly cold. Then place them in pots of suitable size, taking great care to rub the seasoning well over them as you lay them in; because the seasoning is apt to get from the fish when you drain them. Carefully separate the butter which you have strained from the gravy; clarify it, and, when almost cold, pour it into your pots so as to cover your fish completely. If you have not sufficient butter for this purpose you must clarify more, as the fish must be entirely hid from sight. They are fit for use the next day.

Great care must be taken to put them into the pots quite free from the gravy or moisture which they produce.

Another way.

Skin your fish, cleanse them with salt, and wipe them dry. Beat some black pepper, mace, and cloves; mix them with salt, and season your fish with it. Put them in a pan; cover with clarified butter; bake them an hour and season them well; remove the butter after they are baked; take them out of their gravy, and lay them on a coarse cloth to drain. When quite cold, season them again with the same seasoning. Lay them close in the pot; cover them completely with clarified butter; and if your butter is good, they will keep a long time.

Lobsters, to butter.

Put by the tails whole, to be laid in the middle of the dish; cut the meat into large pieces; put in a large piece of butter, and two spoonfuls of Rhenish wine; squeeze in the juice of a lemon, and serve it up.

Lobster Fricassee.

Cut the meat of a lobster into dice; put it in a stewpan with a little veal gravy; let it stew for ten minutes. A little before you send it to table beat up the yolk of an egg in cream: put it to your lobster, stirring it till it simmers. Pepper and salt to your taste. Dish it up very hot, and garnish with lemon.

Lobsters, to hash.

Take the meat out of a boiled lobster as whole as you can. Break all the shells; to these and the remains of the body, the large claws excepted, as they have no goodness in them, put some water, cayenne pepper, salt, and common pepper. Let them stew together till the liquor has a good flavour of the lobster, but observe that there must be very little water, and add two teaspoonfuls of anchovy pickle. Strain through a common sieve; put the meat of the lobster to the gravy; add some good rich melted butter, and send to table. Lobster sauce is made in the same way, only the meat should be cut smaller than for hashing. Hen lobsters are best.

Lobsters, to pot.

Boil four moderate-sized lobsters, take off the tails, and split them. Take out the flesh as whole as possible; pick the meat out of the body and chine; beat it fine, and season with pepper, salt, nutmeg, and mace, and season separately, in the same manner, the tails and claws, which must also be taken out as whole as you can. Clarify a pound of the very finest butter; skim it clean; put in the tails and claws, with what you have beaten, and let it boil a very short time, stirring it all the while lest it should turn. Let it drain through a sieve, but not too much; put it down close in a pot, and, when it is a little cooled, pour over the butter which you drained from it. When quite cold, tie it down. The butter should be the very best, as it mixes with the lobster spawn, &c., and is excellent to eat with the rest or spread upon bread.

Lobsters, to stew.

Half boil two fine lobsters; break the claws and take out the meat as whole as you can; cut the tails in two, and take out the meat; put them in a stewpan, with half a pint of gravy, a gill of white wine, a little beaten mace, cayenne pepper, salt, a spoonful of ketchup, a little anchovy liquor, and a little butter rolled in flour. Cover and stew them gently for twenty minutes. Shake the pan round frequently to prevent the contents from sticking; squeeze in a little lemon. Cut the chines in four; pepper, salt, and broil them. Put the meat and sauce in a dish, and the chines round for garnish.

Lobster Curry Powder.

Eleven ounces of coriander seed, six drachms of cayenne pepper, one ounce of cummin, one ounce and a half of black pepper, one ounce and a half of turmeric, three drachms of cloves, two drachms of cardamoms.

Lobster Patés.

Rub two ounces of butter well into half a pound of flour; add one yolk of an egg and a little water, and make it into a stiff paste. Sheet your paté moulds very thin, fill them with crumbs of bread, and bake lightly. Turn out the crumbs and save them. Cut your lobster small; add to it a little white sauce, and season with pepper and salt. Take care that it is not too thin. Fill your moulds; cover with the crumbs which you saved, and a quarter of an hour before dinner put them into the oven to give them a light colour.

Oyster patés are done the same way.

Lobster Salad.

Boil a cauliflower, pull it in pieces, and put it in a dish with a little pepper, salt, and vinegar. Have four or five hard-boiled eggs, boiled beet-root, small salad, and some anchovies, nicely cleaned and cut in lengths. Put a layer of small salad at the bottom of the dish, then a layer of the cauliflower, then the eggs cut in slices, then the beet, and so on. Take the claws and tail of the lobster, cut as whole as possible, and trim, to be laid on the top. The trimmings and what you can get out may be put in at the time you are laying the cauliflower, &c. in the dish. Make a rich salad sauce with a little elder vinegar in it, and pour it over. Lay the tails and claws on the top, and cross the shreds of the anchovies over them.

Mackarel à la maitre d'hotel.

Boil the fish, and then put it in a stewpan, with a piece of butter and sweet herbs. Set it on the fire till the butter becomes oil.

Mackarel, to boil.

Boil them in salt and water with a little vinegar. Fennel sauce is good to eat with them, and also coddled gooseberries.

Mackarel, to broil.

You may split them or broil them whole; pepper and salt them well. For sauce, scald some mint and fennel, chop them small; then melt some butter and put your herbs in. You may scald some gooseberries and lay over your mackarel.

Mackarel, to collar.

Collar them as eels, only omit the sage, and add sweet herbs, a little lemon-peel, and seasoning to your taste.

Mackarel, to fry.

For frying you may stuff the fish with crumbs of bread, parsley well chopped, lemon-peel grated, pepper and salt, mixed with yolk of egg. Serve up with anchovy or fennel sauce.

Mackarel, to pickle.

Cut the mackarel into four or five pieces; season them very high; make slits with a penknife, put in the seasoning, and fry them in oil to a good brown colour. Drain them very dry; put them into vinegar, if they are to be kept for any time; pour oil on the top.

Mackarel, to pot.

Proceed in the same manner as with eels.

Mackarel, to souse.

Wash and clean your fish: take out the roes, and boil them in salt and water; when enough, take them out and lay them in the dish; pour away half the liquor they were boiled in, and add to the rest of the liquor as much vinegar as will cover them and two or three bay leaves. Let them lie three days before they are eaten.

Mackarel Pie.

Cut the fish into four pieces; season them to your taste with pepper, salt, and a little mace, mixed with a quarter of a pound of beef suet, chopped fine. Put at the bottom and top, and between the layers of fish, a good deal of young parsley, and instead of water a little new milk in the dish for gravy. If you like it rich, warm about a quarter of a pint of cream, which pour in the pie when baked; if not, have boiled a little gravy with the heads. It will take the same time to bake as a veal pie.

Mullet, to boil.

Let them be boiled in salt and water, and, when you think them done enough, pour part of the water from them, and put a pint of red wine, two onions sliced, some nutmeg, salt, and vinegar, beaten mace, a bunch of sweet herbs, and the juice of a lemon. Boil all these well together, with two or three anchovies; put in your fish; and, when they have simmered some time, put them into a dish and strain the sauce over. If you like, shrimps or oysters may be added.

Mullet, to broil.

Let the mullet be scaled and gutted, and cut gashes in their sides; dip them in melted butter, and broil them at a great distance from the fire. Sauce—anchovy, with capers, and a lemon squeezed into it.

Mullet, to fry.

Carefully scale and gut the fish, score them across the back, and then dip them into melted butter. Melt some butter in a stewpan; let it clarify. Fry your mullet in it; when done, lay them on a warm dish. Sauce—anchovy and butter.

Oysters, to stew.

Take a quart of large oysters; strain the liquor from them through a sieve; wash them well, and take off the beards. Put them in a stewpan, and drain the liquor from the settlings. Add to the oysters a quarter of a pound of butter mixed with flour and a gill of white wine, and grate in a little nutmeg with a gill of cream. Keep them stirred till they are quite thick and smooth. Lay sippets at the bottom of the dish; pour in your oysters, and lay fried sippets all round.

Another way.

Put a quarter of a pound of butter into a clean stewpan, and let it boil. Strain a pint of oysters from their liquor; put them into the butter; and let them stew with some parsley minced small, a little shalot shred small, and the yolks of three eggs well beaten up with the liquor strained from the oysters. Put all these together into the stewpan with half a pound more butter; shake it and stew them a little; if too much, you make the oysters hard.

Oysters, ragout of.

Twenty-five oysters, half a table-spoonful of soy, double the quantity of vinegar, a piece of butter, and a little pepper, salt, and flour.

Oysters, to pickle.

Blanch the oysters, and strain off the liquor; wash the oysters in three or four waters; put them into a stewpan, with their liquor and half a pint of white wine vinegar, two onions sliced thin, a little parsley and thyme, a blade of mace, six cloves, Jamaica pepper, a dozen corns of white pepper, and salt according to your taste. Boil up two or three minutes; let them stand till cold; then put them into a dish, and pour the liquor over them.

Oyster Patés. No. 1.

Stew the oysters in their own liquor, but do not let them be too much done; beard them; take a table-spoonful of pickled mushrooms, wash them in two or three cold waters to get out the vinegar; then cut each mushroom into four, and fry them in a little butter dusted over with flour. Take three table-spoonfuls of veal jelly, and two spoonfuls of cream; let it boil, stirring all the while; add a small bit of butter. Season with a pinch of salt, and one of cayenne pepper. Throw the oysters, which you have kept warm in a cloth near the fire, into the sauce; see that it is all hot; then have the patés ready, fill them with the oysters and sauce, and put a top on each. When the paste of oyster patés is done, remove the tops gently and cleanly with a knife; take out the flaky part of the paste inside and from the inside of the top; cut six little pieces of bread square so as to fill the inside; lay on the top of the paste. Then place them on a sheet of paper in a dish, and put them before the fire, covering them with a cloth to keep them hot. When you are going to serve them take out the piece of bread, and fill the patés with the oysters and sauce.

Oyster Patés. No. 2.

Spread some puff-paste about half an inch thick. Cut out six pieces with a small tea-cup. Rub a baking sheet over with a brush dipped in water, and put the patés on it at a little distance from each other. Glaze them thoroughly with the yolk and white of egg mixed up; open a hole at the top of each with a small knife; cut six tops of the size of a crown-piece, and place them lightly on the patés. Let them be baked, and when done remove the tops, and place the crust on paper till ready to serve up; then fill them with oysters (as described in the preceding recipe) put the tops over them, and dish them upon a folded napkin.

Oyster Patés. No. 3.

Parboil your oysters, and strain them from their liquor, wash the beard, and cut them in flour. Put them in a stewpan, with an ounce of butter rolled in flour, half a gill of cream, and a little grated lemon-peel, if liked. Free the oyster liquor from sediment, reduce it by boiling to one half; add cayenne pepper and salt. Stir it over the fire, and fill your patés.

Oyster Loaves.

Cut out the crumb of three French rolls; lay them before the fire till they are hot through, turning them often. Melt half a pound of butter; put some into the loaves; put on their tops, and boil them till they are buttered quite through. Then take a pint of oysters, stewed with half a pint of water, one anchovy, a little pepper and salt, a quarter of a pound of butter, and as much sauce as will make your sauce thick. Give it a boil. Put as many oysters into your loaves as will go in; pour the rest of the sauce all over the loaves in the dish in which they are served up.

Oyster Pie.

Beard the oysters; scald and strain them from their liquor, and season the liquor with pepper, salt, and anchovy, a lump of butter, and bread crumbs. Boil up to melt the anchovies; then just heat your oysters in it; put them all together into your pie-dish, and cover them with a puff-paste.

If you put your oysters into a fresh pie, you must cover them at the top with crisped crumbs of bread; add more to the savouring if you like it.

Perch, to fricassee.

Boil the perch, and strip them of the bones; half cover them with white wine; put in two or three anchovies, a little pepper and salt, and warm it over the fire. Put in a little parsley and onions, with yolks of eggs well beaten. Toss it together; put in a little thick butter; and serve it up.

Pike, to dress.

If you would serve it as a first dish, do not scale it; take off the gills, and, having gutted it, boil it in court bouillon, as a side-dish, or *entrée*. It may be served in many ways. Cut it into pieces, and put it into a stewpan, with a bit of butter, a bunch of all sorts of sweet herbs, and some mushrooms; turn it a few times over the fire, and shake in a little flour; moisten it with some good broth and a pint of white wine, and set it over a brisk fire. When it is done, add a trifle of salt and cayenne pepper, the yolk of three eggs, and half a pint of cream, stirring it till well mixed. Serve up hot.

Pike stuffed, to boil.

Clean a large pike; take out the gills; prepare a stuffing with finely grated bread, all sorts of sweet-herbs, particularly thyme, some onions, grated lemon-peel, oysters chopped small, a piece of butter, the boiled yolk of two eggs, and a sufficient quantity of suet to hold the ingredients together. Put them into the fish, and sew it up. Turn the tail into the mouth, and boil it in pump water, with two spoonfuls of vinegar and a handful of salt. It will take forty minutes to boil, if a large fish.

Pike, to boil, à-la-Française.

Wash well, clean, and scale a large pike, and cut it into three pieces; boil an equal quantity of white wine and water with lemon-peel, and when the liquor boils put your pike in, with a handful of salt. When done, lay it on sippets, and stick it with bits of fried bread. Sauce—melted butter, with slices of lemon in it, the yolks of three eggs, and some grated nutmeg. Pour your sauce over the pike, and serve it up.

Pike, to broil.

Split it, and scotch it with a knife on the outside; season it with salt; put the gridiron on a clear fire, make it very hot, then lay on the pike; baste it with butter, turn it often, and, when broiled crisp and stiff put it into a dish, and serve it up with butter and the juice of lemons, or white wine vinegar. Garnish with slices of oranges or lemons.

Pike in Court Bouillon.

Scale and well wash your pike; lay it in a pan; pour vinegar and salt over it; let it lie for an hour, then take it out, season with pepper, a little salt, sweet herbs, cloves, and a bay leaf, with a piece of butter. Wrap it up in a napkin, and put it into a stewpan, with some white wine, a lemon sliced, a little verjuice, nutmeg, cloves, and a bay leaf. Let this liquor boil very fast; put in the pike, and when done lay it on a warm dish, and strain the liquor into a saucepan; add to it an anchovy washed and boned, a few capers, a little water, and a piece of butter rolled in flour: let these simmer till of proper thickness, and pour them over the fish.

Pike Fricandeau.

Cut a pike in several pieces, according to its size, after having scaled, gutted, and washed, it. Lard all the upper part with bacon cut small, and put it into a stewpan with a glass of red wine (or white wine if for white sauce) some good broth, a bunch of sweet-herbs, and some lean veal cut into dice. When it is stewed and the sauce strained off, complete it in the manner of any other fricandeau; putting a good sauce under it, either brown or white, as you chuse.

Pike, German way of dressing—delicious!

Take a pike of moderate size; when well washed and cleansed, split it down the back, close to the bone, in two flat pieces. Set it over the fire in a stewpan with salt and water; half boil it. Take it out; scale it; put it into the stewpan again, with a very little water, and some mushrooms, truffles, and morels, an equal quantity, cut small; add a bunch of sweet herbs. Let it stew very gently, closely covered, over a very slow fire, or the fish will break; when it is almost done, take out the herbs, put in a cupful of capers, chopped small, three anchovies split and shred fine, a piece of butter rolled in flour, and a table-spoonful of grated Parmesan cheese. Pour in a pint of white wine, and cover the stewpan quite close. When the ingredients are mixed, and the fish quite done, lay it in a warm dish, and pour the sauce over it.

Pike, to pot.

After scaling the fish, cut off the head, split it, take out the back-bone, and strew it over with bay salt and pepper. Cover and bake it; lay it on a coarse cloth to drain, and when cold put it in a pot that will just hold it, and cover with clarified butter.

If not well drained from the gravy it will not keep.

Pike, to roast.

Scale and slash the fish from head to tail; lard it with the flesh of eels rolled up in sweet-herbs and seasoning; fill it with fish and forced meat. Roast it at length; baste and bread it; make the sauce of drawn butter, anchovies, the roe and liver, with mushrooms, capers, and oysters. Ornament with sliced lemon.

Pike au Souvenir.

Wash a large pike; gut and dry it; make a forcemeat with eel, anchovy, whiting, pepper, salt, suet, thyme, bread crumbs, parsley, and a bit of shalot, mixed with the yolks of eggs; fill the inside of the fish with this meat; sew it up; after which draw with your packing-needle a piece of packthread through the eyes of the pike, through the middle and the tail also in the form of S; wash it over with the yolk of an egg, and strew it with the crumbs of bread. Roast or bake it with a caul over it. Sauce—melted butter and capers.

Pike à la Tatare, or in the Tartar fashion.

Clean your pike; gut and scale it; cut it into bits, and lay it in oil, with salt, cayenne pepper, parsley, scallions, mushrooms, two shalots, the whole shred very fine; grate bread over it and lay it upon the gridiron, basting it, while broiling, with the rest of the oil. When it is done of a good colour, serve it in a dry dish, with sauce *à la remoulade* [see Sauces] in a sauce-boat.

Fresh Salmon, to dress.

Cut it in slices, steep it in a little sweet butter, salt and pepper, and broil it, basting it with butter while doing. When done, serve over it any of the fish sauces, as described (see the Sauces), or you may serve it with court bouillon, which will do for all kinds of fish whatever.

Salmon, to dress en caisses, *that is, in small paper cases.*

Take two slices of fresh salmon, about the thickness of half a finger; steep it an hour in sweet butter with mushrooms, a clove of garlic, and a shalot, all shred fine, half a laurel-leaf, thyme, and basil, reduced to a fine powder, salt, and whole pepper. Then make a neat paper box to contain your salmon; rub the outside of it with butter, and put the salmon with all its seasoning and covered with grated bread into it; do it in an oven, or put the dish upon a stove, and, when the salmon is done, brown it with a salamander. When you serve it, squeeze in the juice of a large lemon. If you serve it with Spanish sauce, the fat must be taken off the salmon before you put in the sauce.

Salmon à la Poële, or done on the Stove.

Put three or four slices of fillet of veal, and two or three of ham, having carefully cut off the fat of both, at the bottom of a stewpan, just the size of the salmon you would serve. Lay the salmon upon it, and cover it with thin slices of bacon, adding a bunch of parsley, scallions, two cloves of garlic, and three shalots. Boil it gently over a moderate stove fire, a quarter of an hour; moisten it with a glass of champagne, or fine white wine; let it continue to stew slowly till thoroughly done; and the moment before you serve it strain off the sauce, laying the salmon in a hot dish. Add to the sauce five or six spoonfuls of cullis; let it boil up two or three times, and then pour it over the salmon, and serve up.

Scallops.

Pick the scallops, and wash them extremely clean; make them very dry. Flour them a very little. Fry them of a fine light brown. Make a nice, strong, light sauce of veal and a little ham; thicken a very little, and gently stew the scallops in it for half an hour.

Shrimps, to pot.

Pick the finest shrimps you can procure; season them with a little mace beaten fine, and pepper and salt to your taste. Add a little cold butter. Pound all together in a mortar till it becomes a paste. Put it into small pots, and pour over it clarified butter.

Another way.

To a quart of pickled shrimps put two ounces of fresh butter, and stew them over a moderate fire, stirring them about. Add to them while on the fire twelve white peppercorns and two blades of mace, beaten very fine, and a very little salt.—Let them stew a quarter of an hour: when done, put them down close in pots, and pour clarified butter over them when cold.

Smelts, to fry.

Dry and rub them with yolk of egg; flour or strew some fine bread crumbs on them; when fried, lay them in the dish with their tails in the middle of it. Anchovy sauce.

Smelts, to pickle.

Take a quarter of a peck of smelts, and put them into a jar, and beat very fine half an ounce of nutmegs, and the same quantity of saltpetre and of pepper, a quarter of an ounce of mace, and a quarter of a pound of common salt. Wash the fish; clean gut them, after which lay them in rows in a jar or pan; over every layer of smelts strew your seasoning, with some bay-leaves, and pour on boiled red wine sufficient to cover them. Put a plate or a cover over, and when cold tie them down close.

Smelts, to pot.

Clean the inside of the fish, and season them with salt, pounded mace, and pepper. Bake them, and when nearly cold lay them upon a cloth; then put them into pots, taking off the butter from the gravy; clarify it with more butter, and pour it on them.

Soles, to boil.

The soles should be boiled in salt and water. Anchovy sauce.

Soles, to boil, à-la-Française.

Put a quart of water and half a pint of vinegar into an earthen dish; skin and clean a pair of soles; put them into vinegar and water, let them remain there for two hours. Dry them with a cloth, and put them into a stewpan, with a pint of wine, a quarter of a pint of water, a little sweet marjoram, a very little thyme, an onion stuck with four cloves, and winter savory. Sprinkle a very little bay salt, covering them close. Let them simmer gently till they are done; then take them out, and lay them in a warm dish before the fire. Put into the liquor, after it is strained, a piece of butter rolled in flour; let it boil till of a proper thickness; lay your soles in the dish, and pour the sauce over them.

A small turbot or any flat fish may be done the same way.

Soles, to stew.

Cut and skin the soles, and half fry them; have ready the quantity you like of half white wine and half water, mixed with some gravy, one whole onion, and a little whole pepper. Stew them all together, with a little shred lemon, and a few mushrooms. When they are done enough, thicken the sauce with good butter, and serve it up.

Water Souchi.

Put on a kettle of water with a good deal of salt in it, and a good many parsley roots; keep it skimmed very clean, and when it boils up throw in your perch or whatever fish you use for the purpose. When sufficiently boiled, take them up and serve them hot. Have ready a pint or more of water, in which parsley roots have been boiled, till it has acquired a very strong flavour, and when the fish are dished throw some of this liquor over them. The Dutch sauce for them is made thus:—To a pint of white wine vinegar add a blade or two of mace; let it stew gently by the fire, and, when the vinegar is sufficiently flavoured by the mace, put into it about a pound of butter. Shake the saucepan now and then, and, when the butter is quite melted, make all exceedingly hot; have ready the yolks of four good eggs beaten up. You must continue beating them while another person gently pours to them the boiling vinegar by degrees, lest they should curdle; and continue stirring them all the while. Set it over a gentle fire, still continuing to stir until it is very hot and of the thickness you desire; then serve it.

Sprats, to bake.

Wipe your sprats with a clean cloth; rub them with pepper and salt, and lay them in a pan. Bruise a pennyworth of cochineal; put it into the vinegar, and pour it over the sprats with some bay-leaves. Tie them down close with coarse paper in a deep brown pan, and set them in the oven all night. They eat very fine cold.

You may put to them a pint of vinegar, half a pint of red wine, and spices if you like it; but they eat very well without.

Sturgeon, to roast.

Put a walnut-sized bit of butter (or more if it is a large fish), rolled in flour, in a stewpan, with sweet-herbs, cloves, a gill of water, and a spoonful of vinegar; stir it over the fire, and when it is lukewarm take it off, and put in your sturgeon to steep. When it has been a sufficient time to take the flavour of the herbs, roast it, and when done, serve it with court bouillon, or any other fish sauce.

Turbot, to dress.

Wipe your turbot very dry, then take a deep stewpan, put in the fish, with two bay-leaves, a handful of parsley, a large onion stuck with cloves, some salt, and cayenne; heat a pint of white wine boiling hot, and pour it upon the turbot; then strain in some very strong veal gravy, (made from your stock jelly,) more than will cover it; set it over a stove, and let it simmer very gently, that the full strength of the ingredients may be infused into it. When it is quite done, put it on a hot dish; strain the gravy into a saucepan, with some butter and flour to thicken it.

Plaice, dabs, and flounders, may be dressed in the same way.

Turbot, plain boiled.

Make a brine with two handfuls of salt in a gallon of water, let the turbot lie in it two hours before it is to be boiled; then set on a fish-kettle, with water enough to cover it, and about half a pint of vinegar, or less if the turbot is small; put in a piece of horseradish; when the water boils put in the turbot, the white side uppermost, on a fish-plate; let it be done enough, but not too much, which will be easily known by the look. A small one will take twenty minutes, a large one half an hour. Then take it up, and set it on a fish-plate to drain, before it is laid in the dish. See that it is served quite dry. Sauce—lobster and white sauce.

Turbot, to boil.

Put the turbot into a kettle, with white wine vinegar and lemon; season with salt and onions; add to these water. Boil it over a gentle fire, skimming it very clean. Garnish with slices of lemon on the top.

Turbot, to boil in Gravy.

Wash and well dry a middling sized turbot; put it with two bay-leaves into a deep stew-dish, with some cloves, a handful of parsley, a large onion, and some salt and pepper, add a pint of boiling hot white wine, strain in some strong veal gravy that will more than cover the fish, and remove it on one side that the ingredients may be well mixed together. Lay it on a hot dish, strain the gravy into a saucepan with some butter and flour, pour a little over the fish, and put the remainder in a sauce terrine.

Turbot, to boil in Court Bouillon, with Capers.

Be very particular in washing and drying your turbot. Take thyme, parsley, sweet-herbs of all sorts, minced very fine, and one large onion sliced; put them into a stewpan, then lay in the turbot—the stewpan should be just large enough to hold the fish—strew over the fish the same herbs that are under it, with some chives and a little sweet basil; pour in an equal quantity of white wine and white wine vinegar, till the fish is completely covered; strew in a little bay salt with some pepper. Set the stewpan over a stove, with a very gentle fire, increasing the heat by degrees, till it is done sufficiently. Take it off the fire, but do not take the turbot out: let it stand on the side of the stove. Set a saucepan on the fire, with a pound of butter and two anchovies, split, boned, and carefully cleansed, two large spoonfuls of capers cut small, some chives whole, and a little cayenne, nutmeg grated, a little flour, a spoonful of vinegar, and a little broth. Set the saucepan over the stove, keep shaking it round for some time, and then leave it at the side of the stove. Take up the stewpan in which is the turbot, and set it on the stove to make it quite hot; then put it in a deep dish; and, having warmed the sauce, pour it over it, and serve up.

Soles, flounders, plaice, &c. are all excellent dressed in the same way.

Turbot, to fry.

It must be a small turbot. Cut it across, as if it were ribbed; when it is quite dry, flour it, and put it into a large frying-pan with boiling butter enough to cover it; fry it brown, then drain it. Put in enough claret to cover it, two anchovies, salt, a scruple of nutmeg and ginger, and let it stew slowly till half the liquor is wasted; then take it out, and put in a piece of butter, of the size of a walnut, rolled in flour, and a lemon minced, juice and all. Let these ingredients simmer till of a proper thickness. Rub a hot dish with an eschalot or onion; pour the sauce in, and lay the turbot carefully in the midst.

Turbot or Barbel, glazed.

Lard the upper part of your turbot or barbel with fine bacon. Let it simmer slowly between slices of ham, with a little champagne, or fine white, and a bunch of sweet-herbs. Put into another stewpan part of a fillet of veal, cut into dice, with one slice of ham; stew them with some fine cullis, till the sauce is reduced to a thick gravy. When thoroughly done, strain it off before you serve it, and, with a feather, put it over your turbot to glaze it. Then pour some good cullis into the stewpan, and toss it up as a sauce to serve in the dish, adding the juice of a lemon.

Turbot, to dress en gras, *or in a rich fashion.*

Put into a stewpan a small quantity of broth, several slices of veal, and an equal quantity of ham, a little cayenne, and a bunch of sweet-herbs. Let it stew over a very slow stove, and add a glass of champagne. When this is completely done, serve it with any of the sauces, named in the article Sauces, added to its own.

Turbot or Barbel, to dress en maigre, *or in a lean fashion.*

Put into a stewpan a large handful of salt, a pint of water, a clove of garlic, onions, and all sorts of sweet kitchen herbs, the greater variety the better, only an equal quantity of each. Boil the whole half an hour over a slow fire; let it settle. Pour off the clear part of the sauce, and strain it through a sieve; then put twice as much rich milk as there is of the brine, and put the fish in it over a very slow fire, letting it simmer only. When your turbot is done, pour over it any of the sauces named as being proper for fish in the article Sauces.

Turtle, to dress.

After having killed the turtle, divide the back and belly, cleaning it well from the blood in four or five waters, with some salt; take away the fins from the back, and scrape and scald them well from the scales; then put the meat into the saucepan, with a little salt and water just to cover it; stew it, and keep skimming it very clean all the while it is stewing. Should the turtle be a large one, put a bottle of white wine; if a small one, half that quantity. It must be stewed an hour and a half before you put in the wine, and the scum have done rising; for the wine being put in before turns it hard; and, while it is stewing, put an onion or two shred fine, with a little parsley, thyme, salt, and black pepper. After it has stewed tender, take it out of the saucepan, and cut it into small pieces; let the back shell be well washed clean from the blood, and rub it with salt, pepper, thyme, parsley, and onions, shred fine, mixed well together; put a layer of seasoning into the shell, and lay on your meat, and so continue till the shell is filled, covering it with seasoning. If a large turtle, two pounds of butter must be cut into bits, and laid between the seasoning and the meat. You must thicken the soup with butter rolled in flour. An hour and a half is requisite for a large turtle.

Whiting, to dry.

Take the whiting when they come fresh in, and lay them in salt and water about four hours, the water not being too salt. Hang them up by the tails two days near a fire, after which, skin and broil them.

MADE DISHES.

Asparagus forced in French Rolls.

TAKE out the crumb of three French rolls, by first cutting off a piece of the top crust; but be careful to cut it so neatly that the crust fits the place again. Fry the rolls brown in fresh butter. Take a pint of cream, the yolks of six eggs beaten fine, a little salt and nutmeg; stir them well together over a slow fire until the mixture begins to be thick. Have ready a hundred of small asparagus boiled; save tops enough to stick in the rolls; the rest cut small and put into the cream; fill the rolls with it. Before you fry the rolls, make holes thick in the top crust to stick the asparagus in; then lay on the piece of crust, and stick it with asparagus as if it was growing.

Eggs, to dress.

Boil or poach them in the common way. Serve them on a piece of buttered toast, or on stewed spinach.

Eggs buttered. No. 1.

Take the yolks and whites; set them over the fire with a bit of butter, and a little pepper and salt; stir them a minute or two. When they become rather thick and a little turned in small lumps, pour them on a buttered toast.

Eggs buttered. No. 2.

Put a lump of butter, of the size of a walnut; beat up two eggs; add a little cream, and put in the stewpan, stirring them till they are hot. Add pepper and salt, and lay them on toast.

Eggs buttered. No. 3.

Beat the eggs well together with about three spoonfuls of cream and a little salt; set the mass over a slow fire, stirring till it becomes thick, without boiling, and have a toast ready buttered to pour it upon.

Milk with a little butter, about the size of a walnut, may be used instead of the cream.

Eggs, Scotch.

Take half a pound of the flesh of a fowl, or of veal, or any white meat (dressed meat will do), mince it very small with half a pound of suet and the crumb of a French roll soaked in cream, a little parsley, plenty of lemon-peel shred very small, a little pepper, salt, and nutmeg; pound all these together, adding a raw egg, till they become a paste. Boil as many eggs as you want very hard; take out the yolks, roll them up in the forcemeat, and make them the size and shape of an egg. Fry them till they are of a light brown, and toss them up in a good brown sauce. Quarter some hard-boiled eggs, and spread them over your dish.

Eggs for second Course.

Boil five eggs quite hard; clear away the shells, cut them in half, take out the yolks, and put the whites into warm water. Pound the yolks in a mortar till they become very fine. Have ready some parsley and a little onion chopped as fine as possible; add these to the yolks, with a pinch of salt and cayenne pepper. Add a sufficient quantity of hot cream to make it into a thick even paste; fill the halves of the whites with this, and keep the whole in hot water. Prepare white sauce; place the eggs on a dish in two rows, the broad part downward; pour the sauce over them, and serve up hot.

Eggs to fry as round as Balls.

Put three pints of clarified butter into a deep stewpan; heat it as hot as for fritters, and stir the butter with a stick till it turns round like a whirlpool. Break an egg into the middle, and turn it round with the stick till it is as hard as a poached egg. The whirling round of the butter makes it as round as a ball. Take it up with a slice; put it in a dish before the fire. Do as many as you want; they will be soft, and keep hot half an hour. Serve on stewed spinach.

Eggs, fricassee of.

Boil the eggs pretty hard; cut them in round slices; make white sauce and pour it over them; lay sippets round your dish, and put a whole yolk in the middle.

Eggs à la Crême.

Boil the eggs, which must be quite fresh, twelve minutes; and throw them into cold water. When cold, take off the shell without breaking the white. Have a little shalot and parsley minced fine and mixed; pass it with a little fresh butter. When done enough, set it to cool. Cut the eggs through the middle; put the whites into warm water; pound the yolks very fine; put them into your stewpan, with a little cream, pepper, and salt. Make the whole very hot, and dish. Two gills of cream will be sufficient for ten eggs.

Ham, essence of.

Take six pounds of ham; cut off all the skin and fat, and cut the lean into slices about an inch thick; lay them in the bottom of a stewpan, with slices of carrots, parsnips, six onions sliced; cover down very close, and set it over a stove. Pour on a pint of veal cullis by degrees, some fresh mushrooms cut in pieces, if to be had, if not, mushroom powder, truffles, morels, two cloves, a basil leaf, parsley, a crust of bread, and a leek. Cover down close, and let it simmer till the meat is quite dissolved. A little of this sauce will flavour any lighter sauce with great zest and delicacy.

Maccaroni in a mould of Pie Crust.

Prepare a paste, as generally made for apple-pies, of an oval shape; put a stout bottom to it and no top; let it bake by the fire till served. Prepare a quarter of a pound of maccaroni, boil it with a little salt and half an ounce of butter; when done, put it in another stewpan with an ounce more of butter, a little grated cheese, and a spoonful of cream. Drain the maccaroni, and toss it till the cheese be well mixed; pour it into a dish; sprinkle some more grated cheese over it, and baste it with a little butter. When ready to be served, put the maccaroni into the paste, and dish it up hot without browning the cheese.

Maccaroni, to dress. No. 1.

Stew one pound of gravy beef to a rich gravy, with turnips and onions, but no carrots; season it high with cayenne, and fine it with whites of eggs. When the gravy is cold, put in the maccaroni; set it on a gentle fire; stir it often that it may not burn, and let it stew an hour and a half. When you serve it up add of Cheshire cheese grated as much as will make the maccaroni relishing.

Maccaroni. No. 2.

Boil two ounces of maccaroni in plenty of water an hour and a half, and drain it through a sieve. Put it into a saucepan, and beat a little bit of butter, some pepper and salt, and as much grated cheese as will give a proper flavour. Put it into the saucepan with the maccaroni, and add two spoonfuls of cream. Set it on the fire, and stew it up. Put it on your dish; strew a little grated cheese over it, and brown with a salamander.

Maccaroni. No. 3.

Boil the maccaroni till tender; cut it in pieces about two inches long; put it into either white or brown sauce, and let it stew gently for half an hour. Either stir in some grated cheese, or send it in plain. Pepper and salt to your taste.

Maccaroni. No. 4.

Soak a quarter of a pound of maccaroni in milk for two hours; put it into a stewpan, boil it well, and thicken with a little flour and butter. Season it with pepper and salt to your taste; and add three table-spoonfuls of cream. Put it in a dish; add bread crumbs and sliced cheese, and brown with a salamander.

Maccaroni. No. 5.

Set on the fire half a gallon of water; when it boils put into it one pound of maccaroni, with a quarter of a pound of salt; let it boil a quarter of an hour, then strain very dry, put it in a stewpan with a quarter of a pound of fresh butter; let it fry a quarter of an hour longer. Add pepper and grated cheese; stew them together; then put the maccaroni into a terrine, and shake some grated cheese on it. It is very good with a-la-mode beef gravy instead of butter.

Maccaroni. No. 6.

Boil a quarter of a pound of maccaroni till it is quite tender; lay it on a sieve to drain; then put it into a tossing-pan with about a gill of cream and a piece of butter rolled in flour. Boil five minutes, pour it on a plate, and lay Parmesan cheese toasted all over it.

Maccaroni. No. 7.

Break a quarter of a pound of pipe maccaroni into pieces about an inch long, put it into a quart of boiling broth; boil it for three hours; then strain it off from the broth, and make a sauce with a bit of butter, a little flour, some good broth, and a little cream; when it boils add a little Parmesan cheese. Put your maccaroni into the sauce, and just stir it together. Put it on the dish for table, with grated Parmesan cheese over it, and give it a good brown colour with a hot shovel or salamander.

Maccaroni. No. 8.

Boil three ounces of maccaroni in water till quite tender; lay it on a sieve to drain; when dry, put it into a stewpan, over a charcoal fire, with three or four spoonfuls of fresh cream, one ounce of butter, and a little grated Parmesan cheese. Set it over a slow fire till quite hot, but it must not boil; pour it into your hot dish; shake a little of the cheese over the top, and brown with a salamander.

Omelets.

should be fried in a small frying-pan, made for the purpose; with a small quantity of butter. Their great merit is to be thick; therefore use only half the number of whites that you do of yolks of eggs. The following ingredients are the basis of all omelets: parsley, shalot, a portion of sweet-herbs, ham, tongue, anchovy, grated cheese, shrimps, oysters, &c.

Omelet. No. 1.

Slice very thin two onions, about two ounces each; put them in a stewpan with three ounces of butter; keep the pan covered till done, stirring now and then, and, when of a nice brown, stir in as much flour as will produce a stiff paste. Add by degrees as much water or milk as will make it the thickness of good cream, and stew it with pepper and salt; have ready hard-boiled eggs (four or five); you may either shred or cut them in halves or quarters.

Omelet. No. 2.

Beat five eggs lightly together, a small quantity of shalot, shred quite fine; parsley, and a few mushrooms. Fry, and be careful not to let it burn. When done add a little sauce.

Omelet. No. 3.

Break five eggs into a basin; add half a pint of cream, a table-spoonful of flour, a little pounded loaf-sugar, and a little salt. Beat it up with a whisk for five minutes; add candied citron and orange peel; fry it in two ounces of butter.

Omelet. No. 4.

Take six or seven eggs, a gill of good cream, chopped parsley, thyme, a very small quantity, shalot, pepper, salt, and a little grated nutmeg. Put a little butter in your frying-pan, which must be very clean or the omelet will not turn out. When your butter is melted, and your omelet well beat, pour it in, put it on a gentle fire, and as it sets keep moving and mixing it with a spoon. Add a little more butter if required. When it is quite loose from the bottom, turn it over on the dish in which it is to be served.

Omelet. No. 5.

Break eight eggs into an earthen pan, with a little pepper and salt, and water sufficient to dissolve the salt; beat the eggs well. Throw an ounce and a half of fresh butter into a frying-pan; melt it over the fire; pour the eggs into the pan; keep turning them continually, but never let the middle part be over the fire. Gather all the border, and roll it before it is too much done; the middle must be kept hollow. Roll it together before it is served. A little chopped parsley and onions may be mixed with the butter and eggs, and a little shalot or pounded ham.

Omelet. No. 6.

Four eggs, a little scraped beef, cayenne pepper, nutmeg, lemon peel, parsley, burnet, chervil, and onion, all fried in lard or butter.

Asparagus Omelet.

Beat up six eggs, put some cream to them. Boil some asparagus, cut off the green heads, and mix with the eggs; add pepper and salt. Make the pan hot; put in some butter; fry the omelet, and serve it hot.

A French Omelet.

Beat up six eggs; put to them a quarter of a pint of cream, some pepper, salt, and nutmeg; beat them well together. Put a quarter of a pound of butter, made hot, into your omelet-pan, and fry it of a light brown. Double it once, and serve it up plain, or with a white sauce under it. If herbs are preferred, there should be a little parsley shred, and green onion cut very fine, and serve up fried.

Ragout for made dishes.

Boil and blanch some cocks' combs, with sweetbreads sliced and lambs' stones; mix them up in gravy, with sweet-herbs, truffles, mushrooms, oysters, and savoury spice, and use it when you have occasion.

Trouhindella.

Chop fine two pounds of veal, fat and lean together; slice crumb of bread into some warm milk: squeeze it out of the milk and put it to the veal; season with pepper, salt, and nutmeg; make it up in three balls, and fry it in butter half an hour. Put a quart of mutton or veal broth into the pan, and let it stew three quarters of an hour, or till it is reduced to a quarter of a pint of strong gravy.

MEATS AND VEGETABLES.

Artichokes, to fricassee.

Scrape the bottom clean; cut them into large dice, and boil them, but not too soft. Stove them in a little cream, seasoned with pepper and salt; thicken with the yolks of four eggs and melted butter, and serve up.

Bacon, to cure. No. 1.

Use two pounds of common salt; one pound of bay salt; one pound of brown sugar; two ounces of saltpetre; two ounces of ground black pepper.

Bacon, to cure. No. 2.

Take half a pound of saltpetre, or let part of it be petre salt, half a pound of bay salt, and one pound of coarse sugar; pound and mix them well together. Rub this mixture well into the bacon, and cover it completely with common salt. Dry it thoroughly, and keep it well packed in malt dust.

Bacon, to cure. No. 3.

For sixty pounds' weight of pork take three pounds of common salt, half a pound of saltpetre, and half a pound of brown sugar. The sugar must be put on first and well rubbed in, and last of all the common salt. Let the meat lie in salt only a week, and then hang it at a good distance from the fire, but in a place where a fire is constantly kept. When thoroughly dry, remove it into a garret, and there let it remain till wanted for use.

Barbicue.

Cut either the fore quarter or leg of a small pork pig in the shape of a ham; roast it well, and a quarter of an hour before it is enough done, baste it with Madeira wine; then strain the Madeira and gravy in the dripping-pan through a sieve; mix to your taste with cayenne pepper and lemon-juice; and serve it in the dish.

Alamode Beef. No. 1.

Take a piece of the round of beef, fresh and tender; beat it well, and to six pounds of beef put one pound of bacon, cut into large pieces for larding, and season it with pepper, cloves, and salt. Lard your beef, and put it into your stewpan, with a bay-leaf or two, and two or three onions, a bunch of parsley, a little lemon-peel, three spoonfuls of vinegar, and the same quantity of beer. Cover it close, and set it over a gentle charcoal fire; stew it very gently that your liquor may come out; and shake it often to prevent its sticking. As the liquor increases, make your fire a little stronger, and, when enough done, skim off all the fat, and put in a glass of claret. Stew it half an hour longer, and when you take it off your fire squeeze in the juice of a lemon, and serve up. It must stew five hours; and is as good cold as hot.

Alamode Beef. No. 2.

Lard the mouse-buttock with fat bacon, sprinkled with parsley, scallions, mushrooms, truffles, morels, one clove of garlic shred fine, salt, and pepper. Let it stew five or six hours in its own gravy, to which add, when it is about half done, a large spoonful of brandy. It should be done in an earthen vessel just large enough to contain it, and may be served hot or cold.

Alamode Beef. No. 3.

Lard a piece of beef with fat bacon, dipped in pepper, vinegar, allspice, and salt; flour it all over; cut two or three large onions in thin slices; lay them at the bottom of the stewpan with as much butter as will fry your beef; lay it in and brown it all over; turn it frequently. Pour to it as much boiling water as will cover it; add a little lemon-peel, and a bunch of herbs, which must be taken out before done enough; when it has stewed about two hours turn it. When finished, put in some mushrooms or ketchup, and serve up.

Alamode Beef, in the French manner.

Take the best part of the mouse-buttock, between four and seven pounds, larded well with fat bacon, and cut in square pieces the length and thickness of your beef. Before you lard it, take a little mace, six cloves, some pepper and salt, ground all together, and mix it with some parsley, shalot, and a few sweet-herbs; chop them small, roll your bacon in this mixture, and lard your beef. Skewer it well, and tie it close with a string; put two or three slices of fat bacon at the bottom of your stewpan, with three slices of carrot, two onions cut in two, and half a pint of water; put your beef in, and set your stewpan on the fire. After the beef has stewed about ten minutes, add more hot water, till it half covers the meat; let it boil till you feel with your finger that your beef is warm or hot through. Lay two or three slices of fat bacon upon your beef, add a little mace, cloves, pepper, and salt, a few slices of carrot, a small bunch of sweet-herbs, and celery tied together, a little garlic if you like it. Cut a piece of paper, of the size of your cover; well grease it with butter or lard; put it over your pan, cover it close, and let it stew over a very slow fire seven or eight hours. If you like to eat the beef cold, do not uncover the pan till it is so, for it will be the better for it. If you choose to stew a knuckle of veal with the beef, it will add greatly to the flavour.

Rump of Beef, with onions.

Having extracted the bones, tie it compactly in a good shape, and stew it in a pan that will allow for fire at the top. Put in a pint of white wine, some good broth, a slice of veal, two of bacon, or ham, which is better, a large bunch of kitchen herbs, pepper and salt. When the beef is nearly half done, add a good quantity of onions. The beef being thoroughly done, take it out and wipe off the grease; place it in the dish in which it is to be served at table, put the onions round it, and pour over it a good sauce, any that suits your taste.

Rump of Beef, to bake.

Bone a rump of beef; beat it thoroughly with a rolling-pin, till it is very tender; cut off the sinew, and lard it with large pieces of bacon; roll your larding seasoning first—of pepper, salt, and cloves. Lard athwart the meat that it may cut handsomely; then season the meat all over with pepper and salt, and a little brown sugar. Tie it neatly up with packthread across and across, put the top undermost, and place it in an earthen pan. Take all the bones that came out of it, and put them in round and round the beef, so that it cannot stir; then put in half a pound of butter, two bay-leaves, two shalots, and all sorts of seasoning herbs, chopped fine. Cover the top of the pot with coarse paste; put it in a slow oven; let it stand eight hours; take it out, and serve it in the dish in which it is to go to table, with its own juice, and some have additional broth or gravy ready to add to it if it is too dry.

Rump of Beef, cardinal fashion.

Choose a rump of beef of moderate size, say ten or twelve pounds; take out the bones; beat it, and lard it with a pound of the best bacon, mingled with salt and spices, without touching the upper parts. Rub half a quarter of a pound of saltpetre in powder into the meat that it may look red; and put it into a pan with an ounce of juniper-berries a little bruised, a tea-spoonful of brown sugar, a little thyme, basil, and a pound of salt; and there let it remain, the pan being covered close, for eight days. When the meat has taken the salt, wash it in warm water, and put some slices of bacon upon the upper part on that side which is covered with fat, and tie a linen cloth over it with packthread. Let it stew gently five hours, with a pint and a half of red wine, a pint of water, six onions, two cloves of garlic, five carrots, two parsnips, a laurel leaf, thyme, basil, four or five cloves, parsley, and scallions. When it is done, it may be either served up hot, or left to cool in its own liquor, and eaten cold.

Beef, sausage fashion.

Take a slice of beef, about half an inch thick and four or five wide; cut it in two equal parts; beat them well to make them flat, and pare the edges neatly. Mince your parings with beef suet, parsley, onions, mushroom, a shalot, two leaves of basil, and mix them into a forcemeat with the yolks of four eggs. A little minced ham is a great addition. Spread this forcemeat upon the slices of beef, and roll them up in the form of sausages. Tie them with packthread, and stew them in a little broth, a glass of white wine, salt, pepper, an onion stuck with cloves, a carrot, and a parsnip. When they are done, strain off the liquor, and, having skimmed off the fat, reduce it over the fire to the consistence of a sauce; take care that it be not too highly flavoured, and serve it over your sausages, or they may be served on sorrel, spinach, or any other sauce you prefer.

Ribs and Sirloin of Beef.

When the ribs and sirloin are tender, they are commonly roasted, and eaten with their own gravy. To make the sirloin still better, take out the fillet: cut it into thin slices, and put it into a stewpan, with a sauce made with capers, anchovies, mushrooms, a little garlic, truffles, and morels, the whole shred fine, turned a few times over the fire, with a little butter, and moistened with some good cullis. When the sauce is skimmed and seasoned to your taste, put in the fillet with the gravy of the meat, and heat and serve it over the ribs or sirloin.

Rib of Beef, en papillotes, (in paper.)

Cut a rib of beef neatly, and stew it with some broth and a little pepper and salt. When the meat is done enough, reduce the sauce till it sticks to the rib, and then steep the rib in butter, with parsley, scallions, shalots, and mushrooms, shred fine, and a little basil in powder. Wrap the rib, together with its seasoning, in a sheet of white paper, folding the paper round in the form of a curling paper or papillote; grease the outside, and lay it upon the gridiron, on another sheet of greased paper, over a slow fire. When it is done, serve it in the paper.

Brisket of Beef, stewed German Fashion.

Cut three or four pounds of brisket of beef in three or four pieces of equal size, and boil it a few minutes in water; in another pan boil the half of a large cabbage for a full quarter of an hour; stew the meat with a little broth, a bunch of parsley, scallions, a little garlic, thyme, basil, and a laurel-leaf; and an hour afterwards put in the cabbage, cut into three pieces, well squeezed, and tied with packthread, and three large onions. When the whole is nearly done, add four sausages, with a little salt and whole pepper, and let it stew till the sauce is nearly consumed; then take out the meat and vegetables, wipe off the grease, and dish them, putting the beef in the middle, the onions and cabbage round, and the sausages upon it. Strain the sauce through a sieve, and, having skimmed off the fat, serve it over the ragout. The beef will take five hours and a quarter at the least to stew.

Beef, to bake.

Take a buttock of beef; beat it in a mortar; put to it three pounds of bacon cut in small pieces; season with pepper and salt, and mix in the bacon with your hands. Put it into a pot, with some butter and a bunch of sweet-herbs, covering it very close, and let it bake six hours. When enough done, put it into a cloth to strain; then put it again into your pot, and fill it up with butter.

Beef bouilli.

Take the thick part of the brisket of beef, and let it lie in water all night; tie it up well, and put it to boil slowly, with a small faggot of parsley and thyme, a bag of peppercorns and allspice, three or four onions, and roots of different sorts: it will take five or six hours, as it should be very tender.

Take it out, cut the string from it, and either glaze it or sprinkle some dry parsley that has been chopped very fine over it; sprinkle a little flour on the top of it, with gherkin and carrot. The chief sauce for it is *sauce hachée*, which is made thus: a little dressed ham, gherkin, boiled carrot, and the yolk of egg boiled, all chopped fine and put into brown sauce.

Another way.

Take about eight or nine pounds of the middle part of the brisket; put it into your stew-kettle (first letting it hang up for four or five days) with a little whole pepper, salt, and a blade or two of mace, a turnip or two, and an onion, adding about three pints or two quarts of water. Cover it up close, and when it begins to boil skim it; let it stand on a very slow fire, just to keep it simmering. It will take five hours or more before it is done, and during that time you must take the meat out, in order to skim off the fat. When it is quite tender take your stewpan, and brown a little butter and flour, enough to thicken the gravy, which you must put through a colander, first adding sliced carrots and turnips, previously boiled in another pot. You may also, if you choose, put in an anchovy, a little ketchup, and juice of lemon; but these are omitted according to taste. When the gravy is thus prepared, put the meat in again; give it a boil, and dish it up.

Relishing Beef.

Take a round of the best piece of beef and lard it with bacon; half roast it; put it in a stewpan, with some gravy, an onion stuck with cloves, half a pint of white wine, a gill of vinegar, a bunch of sweet-herbs, pepper, cloves, mace, and salt; cover it down very close, and let it only simmer till it is quite tender. Take two ox-palates, two sweetbreads, truffles, morels, artichoke-bottoms, and stew them all together in some good gravy, which pour over the beef. Have ready forcemeat balls fried, made in different shapes; dip some sippets into butter, fry and cut them three-corner-ways, stick them into the meat; lay the balls round the dish.

Beef, to stew.

Take a pound and a half of the fat part of a brisket, with four pounds of stewing beef, cut into pieces; put these into a stewpan, with a little salt, pepper, a bunch of sweet-herbs and onions, stuck with cloves, two or three pieces of carrots, two quarts of water, and half a pint of good small beer. Let the whole stew for four hours; then take some turnips and carrots cut into pieces, a small leek, two or three heads of celery, cut small, and a piece of bread toasted hard. Let these stew all together one hour longer; then put the whole into a terrine, and serve up.

Another way.

Put three pounds of the thin part of the brisket of beef and half a pound of gravy beef in a stewpan, with two quarts of water, a little thyme, marjoram, parsley, whole pepper and salt, a sufficient quantity, and an onion; let it stew six hours or more; then add carrots, turnips, (cut with a machine) and celery cut small, which have all been previously boiled; let the vegetables be stewed with the beef one hour. Just before you take it off the fire, put in some boiled cabbage chopped small, some pickled cucumbers and walnuts sliced, some cucumber liquor, and a little walnut liquor. Thicken the sauce with a lump of butter rolled in flour. Strew the cut vegetables over the top of the meat.

Cold Beef, to dress.

Slice it as thin as possible; slice, also, an onion or shalot; squeeze on it the juice of a lemon or two; then beat it between two plates, as you do cucumbers. When it is very well beaten, and tastes sharp of the lemon, put it into the dish, in which it is to be served; pick out the onion, and strew over it some fine shred parsley and fine bread crumbs; then pour on it oil and mustard well mixed; garnish with sliced lemon.

Cold Boiled Beef, to dress.

When your rump or brisket of beef has been well boiled in plain water, about an hour before you serve it up take it out of the water, and put it in a pot just large enough to contain it. There let it stew, with a little of its own liquor, salt, basil, and laurel; and, having drained, put it into the dish on which it is to be served for table, and pour over it a sauce, which you must have previously ready, made with gravy, salt, whole pepper, and a dash of vinegar, thickened over the stove with the yolks of three eggs or more, according to the size of the beef and the quantity of sauce wanted. Then cover beef and all with finely grated bread; baste it with butter, and brown it with a salamander.

Cold Beef, to pot.

Cut the beef small; add to it some melted butter, two anchovies well washed and boned, a little Jamaica pepper beat very fine. Beat them well together in a marble mortar till the meat is yellow; then put it into pots, and cover it with clarified butter.

Beef Steaks to broil.

When your steak is nearly broiled, chop some large onions, as fine as possible, and cover the steak thickly with it, the last time you turn it, letting it broil till fit to send to table, when the onion should quite cover the steak. Pour good gravy in the dish to moisten it.

Beef Steaks and Oysters.

Put two dozen oysters into a stewpan with their own liquor; when it boils add a spoonful of water; when the oysters are done drain them in a sieve, and let the liquor settle; then pour it off clear into another vessel; beard them, and add a pint of jelly gravy to the liquor; add a piece of butter and two spoonfuls of flour to thicken it. Let this boil fifteen minutes; then throw in the oysters, and let it stand. Take a beef-steak, pare it neatly round, and dress it as usual; when done, lay it on a hot dish, and pour the sauce and oysters over it.

Rump Steaks broiled, with Onion Gravy.

Peel and slice two large onions; put them into a stewpan with two table-spoonfuls of water; set it on a slow fire till the water is boiled away and the onions have become a little brown. Add half a pint of good broth; boil the onions till tender; strain the broth from them, and chop them fine; thicken with flour and butter, and season with mushroom ketchup, pepper, and salt; put the onions in, and boil it gently for five minutes: pour the gravy over a broiled rump-steak.

Beef Steaks, to stew.

Pepper and salt two fine rump steaks; lay them in a stewpan with a few cloves, some mace, an onion, one anchovy, a bundle of sweet herbs, a gill of white wine, and a little butter mixed with flour; cover them close, stew them very gently till they are tender, and shake the pan round often to keep them from sticking. Take them carefully out, flour and fry them of a nice brown in fresh butter, and put them in a dish. In the mean time strain off the gravy from the fat out of the frying-pan, and put it in the sauce, with a dozen oysters blanched, and a little of the oyster liquor; give it a boil up, pour it over the steaks, and garnish with horseradish. You may fry them first and then stew them; put them in a dish, and strain the sauce over them without any oysters, as a common dish.

Another way.

Beat three pounds of rump steaks; put them in a stewpan, with a pint of water, the same quantity of small beer, six cloves, a large onion, a bunch of sweet-herbs, a carrot, a turnip, pepper, and salt. Stew this very gently, closely covered, for four or five hours; but take care the meat does not go to rags, by being done too fast. Take up the meat, and strain the gravy over it. Have turnips cut into balls, and carrots into shapes, and put them over the meat.

Beef Olives.

Take a rump of beef, cut into steaks, about five inches long and not half an inch thick. Lay on some good forcemeat, made with veal; roll them, and tie them round once or twice, to keep them in a neat shape. Mix some crumbs of bread, egg, a little grated nutmeg, pepper and salt; fry them brown; have ready some good gravy, with a few truffles, morels, and mushrooms, boiled together. Pour it into the dish and send them to table, after taking off the string that tied them in shape.

Another way.

Cut steaks from the inside of the sirloin, about an inch thick, six inches long, and four or five broad: beat and rub them over with yolk of egg; strew on bread crumbs, parsley chopped, lemon-peel shred, pepper and salt, and chopped suet. Roll them up tight, skewer them; fry or brown them in a Dutch oven; stew them in some beef broth or gravy until tender. Thicken the gravy with a little flour; add ketchup, and a little lemon juice, and, to enrich it, add pickled mushrooms, hard yolks of eggs, and forcemeat balls.

Pickle for Beef.

To four gallons of water put a sufficient quantity of common salt; when quite dissolved, to bear an egg, four ounces of saltpetre, two ounces of bay salt, and half a pound of coarse sugar. Boil this pickle for twenty minutes, skim it well, and strain it. When quite cold, put in your beef, which should be quite covered with the pickle, and in nine days it will be fit for use; or you may keep it three months, and it will not be too salt. The pickle must be boiled and well skimmed at the end of six weeks, and every month afterwards; it will then keep three months in summer and much longer in winter.

Beef, to salt.

Into four gallons of water put one pound and a half of coarse brown sugar, two ounces of saltpetre, and six pounds of bay salt; boil and skim as long as any scum rises. When cold, put in the meat, which must be quite covered with pickle: once in two months boil up the pickle again, skimming carefully. Add in the boiling two ounces of coarse sugar, half a pound of bay salt, and the same pickle will be good for twelve months. It is incomparable for hung beef, hams, or neats' tongues. When you take them out of this pickle, clean, dry, and put them in a paper bag, and hang them up in a dry place.

Pork may be pickled in the same manner.

Beef, to salt.

Eight pounds of salt, six ounces of saltpetre, one pound and a half of brown sugar, four gallons of water; boil all together, skim and put on the beef when cold; the beef to be kept under the pickle with a weight.

Beef, to dry.

Salt it in the same way as your hams; keep it in your pickle a fortnight or three weeks, according to its size; hang it up to dry for a few days; then have it smoked the same as hams.

Hung Beef. No. 1.

Take a round, ribs, rump, or sirloin; let it lie in common salt for a month, and well cover it with the brine. Rub a little saltpetre over it two or three days before it is hung up; observing, before it is put up to dry, to strew it over with bran or oatmeal, to keep it from the dust; or, which will answer the same purpose, wrap it up in strong coarse paper. It is not to be smoked; only hang it up in the kitchen, and not too near the fire. The time of hanging to dry must be regulated by the quantity of air in which it is suspended, or left to the discretion of the person who has the care of it. The time which it must lie in water before dressing depends upon the driness of the meat. Half boil it in simmering water, and afterwards roast. It must not be cut till cold.

Hung Beef. No. 2.

Take the under-cliff of a small buttock of beef, two ounces of common salt, and one ounce of saltpetre, well beaten together: put to it half a pint of vinegar with a sprig of thyme. Rub the beef with this pickle every morning for six days, and let it lie in it. Then dry it well with a cloth, and hang it up in the chimney for a fortnight. It must be made perfectly dry before it will be fit for eating; it should also be kept in a dry place.

Hung Beef. No. 3.

Take the tenderest part of beef, and let it hang in the cellar as long as you can, taking care that it is not in the least tainted. Take it down, wash it well in sugar and water. Dry six-pennyworth of saltpetre and two pounds of bay salt, and pound them fine; mix with it three large spoonfuls of brown sugar; rub your beef thoroughly with it. Take common salt, sufficient according to the size of the beef to salt it; let it lie closely covered up until the salts are entirely dissolved, which will be in seven or eight days. Turn it every day, the under part uppermost, and so on for a fortnight; then hang it where it may have a little warmth of the fire. It may hang in the kitchen a fortnight. When you use it, boil it in hay and pump water very tender: it will keep boiled two or three months, rubbing it with a greasy cloth, or putting it for two or three minutes into boiling water to take off any mouldiness.

Beef for scraping.

To four pounds of lean buttock of beef take one ounce of saltpetre and some common salt, in which let the meat lie for a month; then hang it to dry for three weeks. Boil it for grating when wanted.

Italian Beef.

Take a round of beef, about fifteen or eighteen pounds; rub it well with three ounces of saltpetre, and let it lie for four hours in it. Then season it very well with beaten mace, pepper, cloves, and salt sufficient; let it then lie in that seasoning for twelve days; wash it well, and put it in the pot in which you intend to bake it, with one pound of suet shred fine, and thrown under and over it. Cover your pot and paste it down: let it stew six hours in its own liquor, and eat it cold.

Red Beef.

Twelve pounds of ribs of beef boned, four ounces of bay salt, three ounces of saltpetre; beat them fine, and mix with half a pound of coarse sugar, two pounds of common salt, and a handful of juniper berries bruised.

Rub the beef well with this mixture, and turn it every day about three weeks or a month; bake it in a coarse paste.

Another way.

Take a piece of brisket of beef, about sixteen or eighteen pounds; make the pickle for it as follows:—saltpetre and bay salt, one pound and a half of each, one pound of coarse brown sugar, and six pounds of common salt; add to these three gallons of water. Set it on the fire and keep it stirring, lest the salts should burn; as it boils skim it well till clear: boil it about an hour and a half. When it is quite cold, put in the beef, and let it lie in a pan that will hold it properly; turn it every day, and let it remain in about a fortnight. Take it out, and just wash it in clean water, and put it into the pot in which you stew it with some weak broth; then add slices of fat bacon, fat of veal, any pieces of fat meat, the more fat the better, especially of veal, also a pint of brandy, a full pint of wine, a handful of bay-leaves, a few cloves, and some blades of mace, about two large carrots, one dozen of large onions, a good bundle of sweet-herbs, some parsley, and two or three turnips. Stew it exceedingly gently for eight hours. The broth should cover the meat while it is stewing, and keep the slices of fat as much over it as you can; the seldomer you uncover the pot the better. When you think it sufficiently tender, which try with your finger, take it off, and, though it may appear tender enough to fall to pieces, it will harden sufficiently when it grows cold. It should remain in the pot just as it is taken off the fire till it is very nearly if not quite cold. It will eat much better for being so left, and you will also not run the risk of breaking the beef in pieces, as you would by removing it whilst hot.

Collar of Beef.

Bone the navel and navel round; make sufficient pickle to cover it, as strong as to bear an egg, with bay salt; beat two ounces of saltpetre very fine, and strew half of it on your beef before you lay it in your pickle. Then lay it in an earthen pan, and press it down in the liquor with a weight, as it must be all covered. Let it remain thus for four or five days, stirring it however once every day. Take it out, let the brine drain from it, lay it on a table, and season it with nutmeg, pepper, cloves, and mace, some parsley, thyme, and sweet marjoram, of each a little, and eight anchovies sliced; roll it up with these like brawn, and bind it quite fast with strong tape. Then put it into a pan, deep enough for it to stand upright; fill the pan with water, and cover it with paste. Make your oven very hot, put it in, and let it remain there five or six hours; then take it out, and, having removed the tape, roll it in a cloth; hang it up till cold. If you think it not salt enough, before you bake it, put a little salt with your spice and herbs, for baking in water abates much of its saltness.

Another.

Salt a flank of beef with white salt, and let it lie for forty-eight hours. Wash it, and hang it in the wind to dry for twenty-four hours. Then take pepper, salt, cloves, saltpetre, all beaten fine, and mix them together; rub the beef all over; roll it up hard, and tie it fast with tape. Put it in a pan, with a few bay-leaves, and four pounds of butter. Cover the pot with rye paste, and bake it with household bread.

Bisquet, to make.

Cut some slips of white paper; butter and place them at the bottom and sides of the pan you make your bisquet in; then cut thin collops of veal, or whatever meat you make it of; lay them on the paper, and cover them with forcemeat. Put in anything else you like, carrots, &c.; close the top with forcemeat and veal, and paper again; put it in the oven or stove, and, when done, and you want to dish it, turn the pan upside down from the dish; take the paper off, and pour good gravy on it.

Boar's Head, to dress whole.

When the head is cut off, the neck part must be boned, and the tongue taken out. The brains also must be taken out on the inside, so as not to break the bone and skin on the outside. When boned, singe the hair off, and clean it; then put it for four or five days into a red pickle made of saltpetre, bay salt, common salt, and coarse brown sugar, rubbing the pickle in every day. When taken out of the pickle, lay the tongue in the centre of the neck or collar; close the meat together as close as you can, and bind it with strong tape up to the ears, the same as you would do brawn; then put it into a pot or kettle, the neck downward, and fill the pot with good broth and Rhenish wine, in the proportion of one bottle of wine to three pints of broth, till it is covered a little above the ears. Season the wine and broth with small bunches of sweet-herbs, such as basil, winter savory, and marjoram, bay-leaves, shalots, celery, carrots, turnips, parsley-roots, with different kinds of spices. Set it over the fire to boil; when it boils, put it on one side to boil gently, till the head is tender. Take it out of the liquor, and put it into an earthen pan; skim all the fat off the liquor; strain it through a sieve into the head; put it by until it is quite cold, and then it will be fit for use.

Brawn, to keep.

Put some bran and three handfuls of salt into a kettle of water; boil and strain it through a sieve, and, when cold, put your brawn into it.

Hog's head like Brawn.

Wash it well; boil it till the bones will come out; when cold, put the inside of the cheek together with salt between; put the ears round the sides. Put the cheeks into a cloth, press them into a sieve, or anything round; lay on a weight for two days. Have ready a pickle of salt and water, with about a pint of malt, boiled together; when cold, put in the head.

Mock Brawn.

Take two pair of neats' feet; boil them very tender, and take the flesh clean from the bones. Boil the belly piece of pork till nearly done, then bone it, and roll the meat of the feet up very tight in the pork. Take a strong cloth, with some coarse tape; roll it round very tight; tie it up in the cloth; boil it till it is so tender that a skewer may go through it; let it be hung in a cloth till it is quite cold; after which put it into some sousing liquor, and keep it for use.

Cabbage, farced.

Take a fine white-heart cabbage, about as big as a quarter of a peck, lay it in water two or three hours, half boil it, put it in a colander to drain, then cut out the heart, but take very great care not to break off any of the outside leaves. Fill it with forcemeat made thus:—take a pound of veal, half a pound of bacon, fat and lean together; cut them small, and beat them fine in a mortar, with the yolks of four eggs boiled hard; season with pepper and salt, a little beaten mace, a very little lemon-peel, some parsley chopped fine, a very little thyme, and three anchovies. When these are beat fine, take the crumb of a stale roll, some mushrooms, either fresh or pickled, and the heart of the cabbage which you cut out. Chop it very fine; mix all together with the yolk of an egg; fill the hollow of the cabbage, and tie it round with thread. Lay some slices of bacon in the bottom of a stewpan, and upon these some thin slices of coarse beef, about one pound: put in the cabbage, cover it close, and let it stew gently over a slow fire, until the bacon begins to stick to the bottom of the pan. Shake in a little flour; then put in a quart of good broth, an onion stuck with cloves, two blades of mace, some whole pepper, a little bundle of sweet-herbs; cover close, and let it stew gently an hour and a half. Put in a glass of red wine, give it a boil, and take it up; lay it in a dish, and strain the gravy over it, untying the packthread first. This is a very good dish, and makes the next day an excellent hash, with a veal steak nicely boiled and laid on it.

Calf's Head.

Scald the hair off; trim and pare it, and make it look as neat as possible. Take out the bones, and have ready palates boiled tender, hard-boiled yolks of eggs, oysters just scalded, and very good forcemeat: stuff all this into the head, and sew it close in a cloth. Boil it gently for full three hours. Make a strong good gravy for sauce. Garnish with fried bacon.

Calf's Head, to dress like Turtle.

The wool must be scalded off in the same manner as the hair is taken off a little pig, which may be done at the butcher's; then wash and parboil it; cut the meat from the bones, and put it in a saucepan, with as much of the broth as will just cover it. Put in half a tea-spoonful of cayenne pepper, and some common pepper and salt, a large onion, and a faggot of sweet-herbs;

take out the herbs and the onion before it breaks. About half an hour before it is done, put three quarters of a pint of white or raisin wine; have ready the yolks of six or eight eggs boiled hard, which you must make into small balls, and put in just before you serve it up. It will take two hours and a half, or perhaps three hours doing, over a slow fire.

Calf's Head, to hash. No. 1.

Let the calf's head be washed dean, and boiled tender; then cut the meat off one half of the head in small slices. To make the sauce, take some parsley, thyme, and a very little onion, let them be chopped fine; then pass them in a stewpan over the fire, with some butter, till tender. Add some flour, a very little pepper and salt, and some good strong broth, according to your quantity of meat; let it boil, then skim it, put the meat into it, and add a little lemon-juice and a little white wine; let all boil together about ten minutes. There may be some force-meat balls added, if liked. The other half of the head must be scored like diamonds, cross and across; then rub it with some oiled butter and yolk of egg; mix some chopped parsley and thyme, pepper, salt, a little nutmeg, and some bread crumbs; strew the head all over with this; broil it a nice light brown, and put it on the hash when dished. Scald the brains, and cut them in four pieces; rub them with yolk of egg, then let them be crumbed, with the same crumbs and herbs as the head was done with, and fried a light brown; lay them round the dish with a few slices of bacon or ham fried. The brains may be done, to be sent up alone on a plate, as follows:—Let the brains be washed and skinned; let them be boiled in broth, about twenty-five minutes; make a little white sauce of some butter, flour, salt, a little cream, and a little good broth; let it just boil; then pick a little green sage, a little parsley picked very small, and scalded till tender; the brains, parsley, and sage, must be strained off, and put into the white sauce, and let it come to a boil, just before you put them on the dish to send up.

Calf's Head, to hash. No. 2.

Take half a calf's head, cover it with water in a large saucepan, and boil it till the meat comes from the bone. Cut it into pieces; put it into some of the liquor in which the head was boiled, and let it stew till it becomes thick. Add a little salt and mace, and put it into a mould.

Calf's Head, to hash. No. 3.

Your calf's head being half boiled and cooled, cut it in thin slices, and fry it in a pan of brown butter; put it into your tossing pan with gravy; stew it till tender; toss it up with burnt butter, or butter rolled in flour. Garnish with forcemeat balls, and fritters, made of the brains, mixed up with eggs, a little cream, a dust of flour, nutmeg, and a little parsley, boiled and chopped fine. Mix them all well together, and fry them in little cakes; put a few bits of bacon and lemon round the dish.

Calf's Head, to hash. No. 4.

Half boil the head; cut it into round pieces; season with nutmeg, salt, pepper, and a large onion. Save all the gravy, put in a pint of white wine, a quarter of a pound of butter, and four spoonfuls of oyster liquor: let it stew with the meat, not too fast: thicken it with a little butter and a dozen of oysters, and, when dished, add some rolled bacon, forcemeat balls, and the brains fried in thin cakes, very brown, and the size of a crown-piece, laid round the dish. Garnish with lemon and pickled mushrooms; lemon pickle is an addition.

Calf's Head, to hash. No. 5.

Have the head well cleaned; boil it well, cut in slices half of the head, and have some good ragout of forcemeat, truffles, mushrooms, morels, and artichoke bottoms, also some veal sweet-herbs. Season your ragout, and throw in your slices, a bit of garlic and parsley, with some thyme, and squeeze a lemon in it, but be cautious to have it skimmed well. Take the other part of the head, and score it like diamonds; season with salt and pepper, and rub it over with an egg and some crumbs of bread. Then broil it, pour the hash into the dish; let the half head lie in the middle, and cut and set off the brains afterwards in slices. Fry bacon, and lay slices round the dish with sliced lemon.

Calf's Head fricassee.

Clean well a calf's head, boil it and cut in square pieces of about an inch; put half a pint of its own liquor, and mix it well with some mushrooms, sweetbreads, yolks of eggs, artichoke bottoms, and cream. Season with nutmeg and mace, and squeeze in a lemon: but serve it up hot.

Calf's Head, to pickle.

Take out the bones and clean the head carefully: wash it well with eggs, seasoning it with pepper, salt, nutmeg, thyme, and parsley. Put some forcemeat on it, and roll it up. Boil it tender; take it up, lay it in sturgeon-pickle for four days; and if you please you may cut it in pieces as you would sturgeon.

Calf's Liver.

Lay it for a few hours in milk, then dry and fry it in butter.

Cauliflowers, with White Sauce.

Boil the cauliflowers in small pieces till tender; drain them in a sieve; when quite dry lay them in a dish; season the sauce with a little pepper and salt, and pour it pretty thick over them.

Celery, to stew.

Cut and trim a dozen heads of celery; put them in cold water to blanch; stew them in a little butter, salt, and water. When done enough they should be quite soft, but not broken. Drain them, and have ready a rich white sauce, the same that is used for boiled chickens, only without truffles or mushrooms; pour this sauce over the celery, and serve hot.

Another way.

Take a dozen white heads of celery, cut about two inches long, wash them clean, and put them in a stewpan, with a pint of gravy, a glass of white wine, a bundle of sweet-herbs, pepper, and salt: cover close, and stew them till they are tender. Then take out the sweet-herbs; put in a piece of butter mixed with flour; let it stew till it is thick, and dish it up.

Celery à la Crême.

Take a dozen white heads of celery, cut about two inches long; wash them very clean, and boil them in water till they are very tender; have ready half a pint of cream, a little butter mixed with flour, a little nutmeg, and salt; boil it up till thick and smooth; put in the celery, give it a toss or two, and dish it up.

Scotch Collops.

Take a piece of the fillet of veal, as much as will cut into fifteen pieces, of the size and thickness of a crown-piece; shake a little flour over it; put a little butter into a frying-pan, and melt it; fry the slices of veal quick till they are brown, and lay them in a dish near the fire. Then prepare a sauce thus: take a little butter in a stewpan and melt it; add a table-spoonful of flour; stir it about till it is as smooth as cream; put in half a pint each of beef and veal jelly, cayenne pepper and salt, a pinch of each, and one glass of white wine, twenty-four pieces of truffles the size of a shilling, and a table-spoonful of mushrooms: wash them thoroughly from vinegar; squeeze the juice of half a lemon; stew the sauce gently for one hour; then throw in the veal, and stew it all together for five minutes. Serve quite hot, laying the veal regularly in the dish.

Another way.

Cut the lean part of a leg of veal into thin collops; beat them with the back of a knife; season with pepper and salt, shred thyme and parsley, and flour them well. Reserve some of the meat to make balls. Taking as much suet as meat, shred it small; then beat it in a mortar; season with pepper, salt, shred herbs, a little shred onion, and a little allspice. Put in an egg or two, according to the quantity. Make balls, and fry them in good dripping;

keep them warm. Then fry your collops with clarified butter, till they are brown enough; and, while they are warming in the pan, put in your sauce, which must be made thus:—have some good glaze, a little white wine, a good piece of butter, and two yolks of eggs. Put your balls to the collops; flour and make them very hot in the pan; put in your sauce, shake them well, and let them boil. If you would have them white, put strong broth instead of glaze and half a pint of cream.

Scotch Collops, brown.

Cut your collops thin and from the fillet. Season them with salt and pepper, and fry them off quick and brown. Brown a piece of butter thickened with flour, and put in some good gravy, mushrooms, morels, truffles, and forcemeat balls, with sweetbread dried. Squeeze in a lemon, and let the whole boil till of a proper thickness. Then put in your collops, but do not let them boil; toss them up quick, and serve up.

Collops, White. No. 1.

Take a small slice of veal, cut thin slices from it, and beat them out very thin: butter a frying-pan very lightly, place them in it, and pass them on the fire, but not to get any colour. Trim them round, and put them into white sauce.

Collops, White. No. 2.

Cut the veal very thin; put it into a stewpan with a piece of butter and one clove of shalot; toss it in a pan for a few minutes. Have ready to put to it some cream, more or less according to the quantity of veal, a piece of butter mixed with flour, the yolk of an egg, a little nutmeg, and a tea-spoonful of lemon-pickle. Stir it over the fire till it is thick enough, but do not let it boil. If you choose forcemeat balls, have them ready boiled in water, and take out the shalot before you dish up: ten minutes will do them.

Collops, White. No. 3.

Hack and cut your collops well; season with pepper and salt, and fry them quick of a pale colour in a little bit of butter. Squeeze in a lemon: put in half a pint of cream and the yolks of four eggs. Toss them up quick, and serve them hot.

Collops, to mince.

Chop some beef as fine as possible; the under part of roasted beef without any fat is best. Put some onions, pepper, and salt to it. Then put a little butter in the frying-pan; when it is melted, put in the meat, and stew it well. Add a cupful of gravy; if you have none, water will do. Just before it is done put in a little vinegar.

Collops of cold beef.

Take off all the fat from the inside of a sirloin of beef; cut it neatly into thin collops, about the size of a crown or half-crown piece, as you like for size, and cut them round. Slice an onion very small; boil the gravy that came from the beef when roasted, first clearing it of all the fat, with a little water; season it with pepper, and, instead of salt, anchovies dissolved in walnut ketchup, or the liquor from pickled walnuts, and a bundle of sweet-herbs. Let this boil before you put in the collops; put them in with a good piece of butter rolled in a little flour; shake it round to thicken it, and let it do no longer than till the collops are thoroughly heated, lest they be hard. This does better than fresh meat. Serve it hot with pickles, or slices of stewed cucumbers, cut round, like the meat, and placed alternately with it round the dish.

Cucumbers, to stew.

Pare twelve cucumbers, and slice them rather thicker than for eating; put them to drain, and lay them in a coarse cloth till dry. Flour and fry them brown in butter; then put to them some gravy, a little claret, some pepper, cloves, and mace; let them stew a little; then roll a bit of butter in flour, and toss them up. A sufficient quantity of onion should be sliced thin, and done like the cucumbers.

Curry Powder, from a Resident in India. No. 1.

Half a pound of coriander seed, two ounces of black pepper, two ounces of cummin seed, one ounce of turmeric, one ounce and half of ground rice: all the above must be finely pounded; add cayenne to your taste. Mix all well together; put it into a dish close before the fire; roast it well for three or four hours; and, when quite cold, put it into a bottle for use.

Curry Powder. No. 2.

Thirteen ounces of coriander seed,* two ounces of fenugreek seed,* (if not liked this may be omitted,) one ounce of cayenne pepper, or powdered capsicums, six ounces of pale-coloured turmeric,* five ounces of black pepper. Pound the whole very fine; set it in a Dutch oven before the fire to dry, turning it often; when cold put it into a dry bottle; cork, and keep it in a dry place. So prepared, curry-powder will keep for many years.

The ingredients marked thus * may be procured at Apothecaries' Hall, or at any wholesale chemist's.

Curry Powder. No. 3.

One pound of turmeric, one pound of coriander seed, one pound of ginger, six ounces of cardamom, four ounces of cummin, one ounce of long pepper, pounded and mixed together. Cayenne pepper may also be added.

Curry, Indian. No. 1.

Curry may be made of chicken, rabbits, lobster, or of any species of fish, flesh, or fowl. Fry the material with onions, as for mulligatawny, a small piece of garlic, eight almonds, and eight sweet chesnuts. Put it all into a stewpan, with a spoonful or two of curry-powder, a large tea-cupful of strong good gravy, and a large piece of butter. Let the whole stew gently till the gravy becomes very thick and is nearly evaporated.

Particular attention should be paid in sending this dish up hot, and always with plenty of rice in a separate dish; most people like pickle with it.

Curry. No. 2.

Chop one or two onions very fine; put them into a stewpan with some butter, and let them remain on a slow fire till they are well done, taking care not to let them burn. Pour off the butter: put in one dessert spoonful of powder and a little gravy; stir it about till it is well mixed; set it on a slow fire till it is all sufficiently done. Put in a little lemon-juice; when nearly done, thicken the gravy with flour. Let the rice be very well picked and afterwards cleansed; it ought to be washed in several waters, and kept in water till it is going to be boiled. Have the meat or fish ready, pat it into the stewpan, and stir it about till it is well mixed. The rice must be boiled twenty minutes quickly, and the scum taken off; the water to be thrown off and the saucepan uncovered till it is dry enough. Meat used for this curry must be previously fried.

Curry. No. 3.

Fry onions, ginger, garlic, and meat, in one ounce of butter, of a light brown; stew it with a table-spoonful of curry-powder and three pints of water, till it comes to a pint and a half. A good half hour before dinner, put in greens, such as brocoli, cauliflower, sliced apple, and mango, the juice of one lemon, grated ginger, and cayenne, with two spoonfuls of cream, and a little flour to thicken it.

Curry. No. 4.

Skin and prepare two chickens as for a fricassee; wash them very clean, and stew them in a pint and a half of water for about five minutes. Strain off the liquor, and put the chickens in a clean dish. Slice three large onions, and fry them in about two ounces of butter. Put in the chickens, and fry them together till they are brown. Take a quarter of an ounce of curry-powder, and salt to your palate, and strew over the chickens while they are frying; then pour in the liquor in which they were first stewed, and let them stew again for half an hour. Add a quarter of a pint of cream and the juice of two lemons. Have rice boiled dry to eat with it. Rabbits do as well as chickens.

Curry. No. 5.

Take two chickens, or in the same proportion of any other kind of flesh, fish, or fowl; cut the meat small; strew a little salt and pepper over it; add a small quantity of onion fried in butter; put one table-spoonful of curry-powder to your meat and onions; mix them well together with about three quarters of a pint of water. Put the whole in a stewpan covered close; let it stew half an hour before you open the pan; then add the juice of two lemons, or an equal quantity of any other souring. Let it stew again till the gravy appears very thick and adheres to the meat. If the meat floats in the gravy, the curry will not be considered as well made. Salt to your palate.

Curry. No. 6.

Mix together a quart of good gravy, two spoonfuls of curry-powder, two of soy, a gill of red wine, a little cayenne pepper, and the juice of a lemon. Cut a breast of veal in square pieces, and put it in a stewpan with a pint of gravy; stew slowly for a quarter of an hour; add the rest of the gravy with the ingredients, and stew till done.

Curry. No. 7.

Take a fowl, fish, or any meat you like; cut it in slices; cut up two good sized onions very fine; half fry your fowl, or meat, with the onions, in a quarter of a pound of butter. Add two table-spoonfuls of curry-powder, fry it a little longer, and stew it well; then add any acid you like, a little salt, and half a pint of water. Let all stew together until the meat is done.

Farcie, to make.

Take the tender part of a fillet of veal, free from sinew, and mince it fine, with a piece of the fat of ham, some chopped thyme, basil, and marjoram, dried, and a little seasoning according to the palate. Put the whole in a stewpan, and keep stirring it till it is warm through; then put it on a sieve to drain. When the liquor has run from it, pound the farcie, while warm, in a mortar, adding the drained liquor, by degrees, till the whole is again absorbed in the meat, which must be pounded very fine. Put it in an earthen pot, and steam it for half an hour with a slice of fat ham; cover over the pot to prevent the steam from getting to it; when cold, pour on some good jelly made of the lean of ham and veal, and take care to pour it on cold (that is, when the jelly is just dissolved,) otherwise it will raise the farcie. When livers are to be had, put a third of them with the ham and veal, as above directed, and the farcie will be better.

Forcemeat, to make. No. 1.

Chop small a pound of veal, parsley, thyme, a small onion, and a pound of beef; grate the inside of three French rolls, and put all these together, with pepper, salt, soup, and nutmeg, seasoning it to your taste; add as many eggs as will make it of a proper stiffness, and roll them into balls.

Forcemeat. No. 2.

Take half a pound of the lean of a leg of veal, with the skin picked off, cut it into small pieces, and mince it very small; shred very fine a pound of beef-suet and grate a nutmeg into both; beat half as much mace into it with cloves, pepper, and salt, a little rosemary, thyme, sweet marjoram, and winter savory. Put all these to the meat in a mortar, and beat all together, till it is smooth and will work easily with your hands, like paste. Break two new laid eggs to some white bread crumbs, and make them into a paste with your hands, frying it in butter. If you choose, leave out the herbs.

Forcemeat. No. 3.

A pound of veal, full its weight in beef suet, and a bit of bacon, shred all together; beat it in a mortar very fine; season with sweet-herbs, pepper, and salt. When you roll it up to fry, add the yolks of two or three eggs to bind it; you may add oysters or marrow.

Fricandeau.

Take a piece of veal next to the udder; separate the skin, and flatten the meat on a clean cloth; make slits in the bottom part, that it may soak up seasoning, and lard the top very thick and even. Take a stewpan that will receive the veal without confining it; put at the bottom three carrots cut in slices, two large onions sliced, a bunch of parsley, the roots cut small, a little mace, pepper, thyme, and a bay-leaf; then lay some slices of very fat bacon, so as entirely to cover the vegetables, and make a pile of bacon in the shape of a tea-cup. Lay the veal over this bacon; powder a little salt over it; then put sufficient broth, and some beef jelly, lowered with warm water, to cover the bottom of the stewpan without reaching the veal. Lay a quantity of fine charcoal hot on the cover of the pan, keeping a very little fire beneath; as soon as it begins to boil, remove the stewpan, and place it over a very slow and equal fire for three hours and a half, removing the fire from the top; baste it frequently with liquor. When it has stewed the proper time, try if it is done by putting in a skewer, which will then go, in and out easily. Put a great quantity of fire again on the top of the stewpan till the bacon of the larding becomes quite firm; next remove the veal, and keep it near the fire; reduce the liquor to deep rich gravy to glaze it, which pour over the top only where it is larded; and, when it is served, put the fricandeau in a dish, and the puré of spinach, which is to be ready according to the receipt given in the proper place, (See Spinach to stew,) to lay round the dish.

Ham, to cure. No. 1.

Take a ham of young pork; sprinkle it with salt, and let it lie twenty-four hours. Having wiped it very dry, rub it well with a pound of coarse brown sugar, a pound of juniper berries, a quarter of a pound of saltpetre, half a pint of bay salt, and three pints of common salt, mixed together, and dried in an iron pot over the fire, stirring them the whole time. After this, take it off the fire, when boiled, and let it lie in an earthen glazed pan three weeks, but it must be often turned in the time, and basted with the brine in which it lies. Then hang it up till it has done dripping; and dry it in a chimney with deal saw-dust and juniper berries.

Ham, to cure. No. 2.

For two hams, take half a pound of bay salt, two ounces of saltpetre, two ounces of sal prunella, half a pound of brown sugar, half a pound of juniper berries, half a pound of common salt; beat them all, and boil them in two quarts of strong beer for half an hour very gently. Leave out one ounce of saltpetre to rub the hams over-night. Put them into the pickle, and let them lie a month or five weeks, basting them every day. Pickle in the winter, and dry in wood smoke; let them hang up the chimney a fortnight.

Ham, to cure. No. 3.

Hang up a ham two days; beat it well on the fleshy side with a rollingpin; rub in an ounce of saltpetre, finely powdered, and let it lie a day. Then mix together an ounce of sal prunella with two large handfuls of common salt, one handful of bay salt, and a pound of coarse sugar, and make them hot in a stewpan. While hot, rub it well in with two handfuls more of common salt; then let it lie till it melts to brine. Turn the meat twice every day for three weeks, and dry it like bacon.

Ham, to cure—the Thorpe way. No. 4.

The following are the proportions for two hams, or pigs' faces: Boil one pound of common salt, three ounces of bay salt, two ounces and a half of saltpetre, and one pound of the coarsest brown sugar, in a quart of strong old beer. When this pickle is cold, well rub the hams or faces with it every day for a fortnight. Smoke them with horse litter for two hours; then hang them to dry in a chimney where wood is burned for a fortnight, after which, hang them in a dry place till wanted for use. They are not so good if used under eight months or after a year old.

Ham, to cure. No. 5.

For one large ham take one pound of coarse sugar, one pound common salt, a quarter of a pound of saltpetre, and two ounces of bay salt, boiled in a quart of strong ale, or porter. When cold put it to your ham; and let it lie in the pickle three weeks, turning the ham every day.

Ham, to cure. No. 6.

Put two ounces of sal prunella, a pound of bay salt, four pounds of white salt, a pound of brown sugar, half a pound of saltpetre, to one gallon of water; boil it a quarter of an hour, keeping, it well skimmed, and, when cold, pour it from the sediment into the vessel in which you steep, and let the hams remain in the pickle about a month; the tongues a fortnight. In the same manner Dutch beef may be made by letting it lie in the pickle for a month, and eight or ten days for collared beef; dry them in a stove or chimney. Tongues may be cured in the same manner.

Ham, to cure. No 7.

Four gallons of spring water, two pounds of bay salt, half a pound of common salt, two pounds of treacle, to be boiled a quarter of an hour, skimmed well, and poured hot on the hams. Let them be turned in the pickle every day, and remain three weeks or a month; tongues may be cured in the same way.

Ham, to cure. No. 8.

One ounce of pepper, two of saltpetre, one pound of bay salt, one ounce of sal prunella, one pound of common salt. Rub these in well, and let the ham lie a week after rubbing; then rub over it one pound of treacle or coarse sugar. Let it lie three weeks longer; take it up, steep it twenty-four hours in cold water, and then hang it up.

Ham, to cure. No. 9.

One pound of common salt, half a pound of bay salt, four ounces of saltpetre, two ounces of black pepper; mix them together, and rub the ham very well for four days, until the whole is dissolved. Then take one pound and a half of treacle and rub on, and let it lie in the pickle one month; turning it once a day. When you dress it, let the water boil before you put it in.

Ham, to cure. No. 10.

Into four gallons of water put one pound and a half of the coarsest sugar, two ounces of saltpetre, and six pounds of common salt; boil it, carefully taking off the scum till it has done rising; then let it stand till cold. Having put the meat into the vessel in which you intend to keep it, pour on the liquor till it is quite covered. If you wish to keep the meat for a long time, it will be necessary once in two or three months to boil the pickle over again, clearing off the scum as it rises, and adding, when boiling, a quarter of a pound of sugar, half a pound of salt, and half an ounce of saltpetre; in this way the pickle will keep good for a year. When you take the meat out of the pickle, dry it well before it is smoked. Hams from fifteen to twenty pounds should lie in pickle twenty-four days; small hams and tongues, fifteen days; a small piece of beef about the same time. Hams and beef will not do in the same pickle together. After the hams are taken out, the pickle must be boiled again before the beef is put in.

The same process may be used for beef and tongues.

Ham, to cure. No. 11.

Mix one pound and a half of salt, one pound and a half of coarse sugar, and one ounce of saltpetre, in one quart of water; set it on the fire, and keep stirring the liquor till it boils. Skim it. When boiled about five minutes take it off, and pour it boiling hot on the leg of pork, which, if not quite covered, must be turned every day. Let it remain in the pickle one month; then hang it in the chimney for six weeks. These proportions will cure a ham of sixteen pounds. When the ham is taken out of the pickle, the liquor may be boiled up again and poured boiling hot upon pigs' faces. After that boil again, and pour it cold upon a piece of beef, which will be excellent. It will then serve cold for pigs' or sheep's tongues, which must be well washed and rubbed in a little of the liquor and left in the remainder.

Ham, to cure. No. 12.

Take a ham of fifteen pounds, and wash it well with a quarter of a pint of vinegar, mixed with a quarter of a pound of the coarsest sugar. Next morning rub it well with three quarters of a pound of bay salt rolled, on the lean part; baste it often every day for fourteen days, and hang it up to dry.

Ham, to cure. No. 13.

Three ounces of saltpetre, bay salt and brown sugar two ounces of each, a small quantity of cochineal; mix them all together, and warm them over the fire. Rub the hams well with it, and cover them over with common salt.

Ham, to cure. No. 14.

Take a quantity of spring water sufficient to cover the meat you design to cure; make the pickle with an equal quantity of bay salt and common salt; add to a pound of each one pound of coarse brown sugar, one ounce of saltpetre, and one ounce of petre-salt; let the pickle be strong enough to bear an egg. If you design to eat the pork in a month or six weeks, it is best not to boil the pickle; if you intend it for the year, the pickle must be boiled and skimmed well until it is perfectly clear; let it be quite cold before you use it. Rub the meat that is to be preserved with some common salt, and let it lie upon a table sloping, to drain out all the blood; wipe it very dry with a coarse cloth before you put it into the pickle. The proportion of the pickle may be this: four pounds of common salt, four pounds of bay salt, three pounds of coarse sugar, two ounces of saltpetre, and two ounces of petre-salt, with a sufficient quantity of spring water to cover what you do, boiled as directed above. Let the hams lie about six weeks in the pickle, and then send them to be smoked. Beef, pork, and tongues, may be cured in the same manner: ribs of beef done in this way are excellent.

Ham, to cure. No. 15.

Wash the ham clean; soak it in pump water for an hour; dry it well, and rub into it the following composition: saltpetre two ounces, bay salt nine ounces, common salt four ounces, lump sugar three ounces; but first beat them separately into a fine powder; mix them together, dry them before the fire, and then rub them into the ham, as hot as the hand can bear it. Then lay the ham sloping on a table; put on it a board with forty or fifty pounds weight; let it remain thus for five days; then turn it, and, if any of the salt is about it, rub it in, and let it remain with the board and weight on it for five days more; this done rub off the salt, &c. When you intend to smoke it, hang the ham in a sugar hogshead, over a chaffing-dish of wood embers; throw on it a handful of juniper-berries, and over that some horse-dung, and cover the cask with a blanket. This may be repeated two or three times the same day, and the ham may be taken out of the hogshead the next morning. The quantity of salt here specified is for a middle sized ham. There should not be a hole cut in the leg, as is customary, to hang it up by, nor should it be soaked in brine. Hams thus cured will keep for three months without smoking, so that the whole quantity for the year may be smoked at the same time. The ham need not be soaked in water before it is used, but only washed clean. Instead of a chaffing-dish of coals to smoke the hams, make a hole in the ground, and therein put the fire; it must not be fierce: be sure to keep the mouth of the hogshead covered with a blanket to retain the smoke.

Westphalia Ham, to cure. No. 1.

Cut a leg of pork to the shape of a Westphalia ham; salt it, and set it on the fire in a skillet till dry, and put to it two ounces of saltpetre finely beaten. The salt must be put on as hot as possible. Let it remain a week in the salt, and then hang it up in the chimney for three weeks or a month. Two ounces of saltpetre will be sufficient for the quantity of salt required for one ham.

Westphalia Ham, to cure. No. 2.

Let the hams be very well pricked with a skewer on the wrong side, hanging them in an airy place as long as they will keep sweet, and with a gallon of saltpetre make a pickle, and keep stirring it till it will bear an egg; boil and skim it and put three pounds of brown sugar to it. Let the hams lie about a month in this pickle, which must be cold when they are put in; turn them every day; dry them with saw-dust and charcoal. The above is the quantity that will do for six hams.

Westphalia Ham, to cure. No. 3.

Rub every ham with four ounces of saltpetre. Next day put bay salt, common salt, and coarse sugar, half a pound of each, into a quart of stale strong beer, adding a small quantity of each of these ingredients for every ham to be made at that time. Boil this pickle, and pour it boiling hot over every ham. Let them lie a fortnight in it, rubbing them well and turning them twice a day. Then smoke the ham for three days and three nights over a fire of saw-dust and horse-litter, fresh made from the stable every night; after which smoke them for a fortnight over a wood fire like other bacon.

Westphalia Ham, to cure. No. 4.

For two hams the following proportions may be observed: wash your hams all over with vinegar, and hang them up for two or three days. Take one pound and a half of the brownest sugar, two ounces of saltpetre, two ounces of bay salt, and a quart of common salt; mix them together; heat them before the fire as hot as you can bear your hand in, and rub it well into the hams before the fire, till they are very tender. Lay them in a tub made long for that purpose, or a butcher's tray, that will hold them both, one laid one way and the other the contrary way, and strew the remainder of the ingredients over them. When the salt begins to melt, add a pint of vinegar, and let them lie three weeks, washing them with the liquor and turning them every day. Dry them in saw-dust smoke; hang them in a cellar; and if they mould it will do them no harm, as these hams require damp and not extreme driness. Juniper-berries thrown into the fire at which they are smoked greatly improve their flavour.

Westphalia Ham, to cure. No. 5.

One pound of common salt, one pound of bay salt, four ounces of saltpetre, two ounces of black pepper; pound them separately, then mix them, and rub the ham very well until the whole is used. Rub one pound of treacle on them; lay them in the pickle one month, turning them every day. The quantity here specified will do for two hams. Before you hang them up, steep them in a pail of water for twelve hours.

Westphalia Ham, to cure. No. 6.

Make a good brine of salt and water, sufficiently strong to bear an egg; boil and skim it clean, and when quite cold rub the meat with sal prunella and saltpetre mixed together. Put it in a vessel, and pour your brine into it; and, when the ham has been in the brine about fourteen days, take it out, drain it, and boil the brine, putting in a little salt, and letting it boil till clear. Skim it, and when cold put in your ham, rubbing it over with saltpetre, &c. as you did at first. Then let your ham again lie in the brine for three weeks longer; afterwards rub it well with bran, and have it dried by a wood fire.

English Hams, to make like Westphalia. No. 1.

Cut your legs of pork like hams; beat them well with a wooden mallet, till they are tender, but great care must be taken not to crack or break the skin, or the hams will be spoiled. To three hams take half a peck of salt, four ounces of saltpetre, and five pounds of coarse brown sugar; break all the lumps, and mix them well together. Rub your hams well with this mixture, and cover them with the rest. Let them lie three days; then hang them up one night, and put as much water to the salt and sugar as you think will cover them; the pickle must be strong enough to bear an egg: boil and strain it, and, when it is cold, pack your hams close, and cover them with the pickle at least an inch and half above their tops. Let them lie for a fortnight; then hang them up one night; the next day rub them well with bran, and hang them in the chimney of a fire-place in which turf, wood, or sawdust is burned. If they are small they will be dry enough in a fortnight; if large, in two or three days more. Then hang them up against a wall near a fire, and not in a damp place. Tongues may be cured in the same manner, and ribs of beef may be put in at the same time with the hams. You must let the beef lie in the pickle three weeks, and take it out when you want to boil it without drying it.

English Hams, to make like Westphalia. No. 2.

Cut off with the legs of young well grown porkers part of the flesh of the hind loin; lay them on either side in cloths, and press out the remaining blood and moisture, laying planks on them with heavy weights, which bring them into form; then salt them well with common salt and sugar finely beaten, and lay them in troughs one upon another, pressed closely down and covered with hyssop. Let them remain thus for a fortnight; then pass through the common salt, and with saltpetre rub them well over, which may be continued three or four days, till they soak. Take them out, and hang them in a close barn or smoke-loft; make a moderate fire under them, if possible of juniper-wood, and let them hang to sweat and dry well. Afterwards hang them up in a dry and airy place to the wind for three or four days, which will remove the ill scent left by the smoke; and wrap them up in sweet hay. To dress them, put them into a kettle of water when it boils; keep them well covered till they are done, and very few can distinguish them from the true Westphalia.

English Hams, to make like Westphalia. No. 3.

Take a ham of fifteen or eighteen pounds weight, two ounces of saltpetre, one pound of coarse sugar, one ounce of petre-salt, one ounce of bay salt, and one ounce of sal prunella, mixed with common salt enough to cover the ham completely. Turn your ham every other day, and let it remain in salt for three weeks. Take it out, rub a little bran over it, and dry it in a wood fire chimney, where a constant fire is kept: it will be fit for eating in a month. The quantity of the above ingredients must be varied according to the size of your ham. Before you dress it soak it over-night in water.

Hams from bacon pigs are better than pork. An onion shred small gives it a good flavour.

Green Hams.

Salt a leg of pork as for boiling, with a little saltpetre to make it red. Let it lie three weeks in salt, and then hang for a month or six weeks; but if longer it is of no consequence. When boiled, stuff with young strawberry leaves and parsley, which must be particularly well washed or they will be gritty.

Ham, to prepare for dressing without soaking.

Put the ham into a coarse sack well tied up, or sew it up in a cloth. Bury it three feet under ground in good mould; there let it remain for three or four days at least. This is an admirable way. The ham eats much mellower and finer than when soaked.

Ham, to dress.

Boil the ham for two hours; take it out and trim it neatly all round; prepare in a stewpan some thin slices of veal, so as to cover the bottom; add to it two bunches of carrots sliced, six large onions, two cloves, two bunches of parsley, a tea-spoonful of cayenne pepper, a pint of beef jelly, a bottle of white wine, and three pints of boiling water. Place the ham in the stewpan, and let it boil an hour and three quarters; then serve it immediately without sauce, preserving the sauce for other use.

Ham, to roast.

Tie or sew up the ham in a coarse cloth, put it into a sack, and bury it three or four feet under ground, for three or four days before you dress it. Wash it in warm water, pare it, and scrape the rind. Spit and lay it down to roast. Into a broad stewpan put a pint of white wine, a quart of good broth, half a pint of the best vinegar, two large onions sliced, a blade of mace, six cloves, some pepper, four bay-leaves, some sweet basil, and a sprig of thyme. Let all these have a boil; and set the liquor under the ham, and baste very frequently with it. When the ham is roasted, take up the pan; skim all the fat off; pour the liquor through a fine sieve; then take off the rind of the ham, and beat up the liquor with a bit of butter; put this sauce under, and serve it.

Ham, entrée of.

Cut a dozen slices of ham; take off the fat entirely; fry them gently in a little butter. Have a good brown rich sauce of gravy; and serve up hot, with pieces of fried bread, cut of a semicircular shape, of the same size as the pieces of ham, and laid between them.

Ham toasts.

Cut slices of dressed ham, and thin slices of bread, or French roll, of the same shape; fry it in clarified butter; make the ham hot in cullis, or good gravy, thickened with a little floured butter. Dish the slices of ham on the toast; squeeze the juice of a Seville orange into the sauce; add a little pepper and salt; and pour it over them.

Ham and Chicken, to pot. Mrs. Vanbrugh's receipt.

Put a layer of ham, then another of the white part of chicken, just as you would any other potted meat, into a pot. When it is cut out, it will shew a very pretty stripe. This is a delicate way of eating ham and chicken.

Another way.

Take as much lean of a boiled ham as you please, and half the quantity of fat; cut it as thin as possible; beat it very fine in a mortar, with a little good oiled butter, beaten mace, pepper, and salt; put part of it into a china pot. Then beat the white part of a fowl with a very little seasoning to qualify the ham. Put a layer of chicken, then one of ham, then another of chicken at the top; press it hard down, and, when it is cold, pour clarified butter over it. When you send it to table in the pot, cut out a thin slice in the form of half a diamond, and lay it round the edge of the pot.

Herb sandwiches.

Take twelve anchovies, washed and cleaned well, and chopped very fine; mix them with half a pound of butter; this must be run through a sieve, with a wooden spoon. With this, butter bread, and make a salad of tarragon and some chives, mustard and cress, chopped very small, and put them upon the bread and butter. Add chicken in slices, if you please, or hard-boiled eggs.

Hog's Puddings, Black. No. 1.

Steep oatmeal in pork or mutton broth, of milk; put to it two handfuls of grated bread, a good quantity of shred herbs, and some pennyroyal: season with salt, pepper, and ginger, and other spices if you please; and to about three quarts of oatmeal put two pounds of beef suet shred small, and as much hog suet as you may think convenient. Add blood enough to make it black, and half a dozen eggs.

Hog's Puddings, Black. No. 2.

To three or four quarts of blood, strained through a sieve while warm, take the crumbs of twelve-pennyworth of bread, four pounds of beef suet not shred too fine, chopped parsley, leeks, and beet; add a little powdered marjoram and mint, half an ounce of black pepper, and salt to your taste. When you fill your skins, mix these ingredients to a proper thickness in the blood; boil them twenty minutes, pricking them as they rise with a needle to prevent their bursting.

Hog's Puddings, Black. No. 3.

Steep a pint of cracked oatmeal in a quart of milk till tender; add a pound of grated bread, pennyroyal, leeks, a little onion cut small, mace, pepper, and salt, to your judgment. Melt some of the leaf of the fat, and cut some of the fat small, according to the quantity made at once; and add blood to make the ingredients of a proper consistence.

Hog's Puddings, White. No. 1.

Take the pith of an ox, and lay it in water for two days, changing the water night and morning. Then dry the pith well in a cloth, and, having scraped off all the skin, beat it well; add a little rose-water till it is very fine and without lumps. Boil a quart or three pints of cream, according to the quantity of pith, with such spices as suit your taste: beat a quarter of a pound of almonds and put to the cream. When it is cold, rub it through a hair sieve; then put the pith to it, with the yolks of eight or nine eggs, some sack, and the marrow of four bones shred small; some sweetmeats if you like, and sugar to your taste: if marrow cannot be procured suet will do. The best spices to put into the cream are nutmeg, mace, and cinnamon; but very little of the last.

Hog's Puddings, White. No. 2.

Take a quart of cream and fourteen eggs, leaving out half the whites; beat them but a little, and when the cream boils up put in the eggs; keep them stirring on a gentle fire till the whole is a thick curd. When it is almost cold, put in a pound of grated bread, two pounds of suet shred small, having a little salt mixed with it, half a pound of almonds well beaten in orange-flower water, two nutmegs grated, some citron cut small, and sugar to your taste.

Hog's Puddings, White. No. 3.

Take two pounds of grated bread; one pint and a half of cream; two pounds of beef suet and marrow; half a pound of blanched almonds, beat fine with a gill of brandy; a little rose-water; mace, cloves, and nutmeg, pounded, a quarter of an ounce; half a pound of currants, well picked and dried; ten eggs, leaving out half the whites; mix all these together, and boil them half an hour.

Kabob, an India ragout.

This dish may be made of any meat, but mutton is the best. Take a slice from a tender piece, not sinewy, a slice of ginger, and a slice of onion, put them on a silver skewer alternately, and lay them in a stewpan, in a little plain gravy. This is the kabob. Take rice and split peas, twice as much rice as peas; boil them thoroughly together, coloured with a little turmeric, and serve them up separately or together. The ginger must be steeped overnight, that you may be able to cut it.

Another way.

To make the kabob which is usually served up with pilaw, take a lean piece of mutton, and leave not a grain of fat or skin upon it; pound it in a mortar as for forcemeat; add half a clove of garlic and a spoonful or more of curry-powder, according to the size of the piece of meat, and the yolk of an egg. Mix all well together; make it into small cakes; fry it of a light brown, and put it round the pilaw.

Leg of Lamb, to boil.

Divide the leg from the loin of a hind quarter of lamb; slit the skin off the leg, and cut out the flesh of one side of it, and chop this flesh very small; add an equal quantity of shred beef suet and some sweet-herbs shred small; season with nutmeg, pepper, and salt; break into it two eggs. Mix all well together, put it into the leg, sew it up, and boil it. Chop the loin into steaks, and fry them, and, when the leg is boiled enough, lay the steaks round it. Take some white wine, anchovies, nutmeg, and a quarter of a pound of butter; thicken with the yolks of two eggs; pour it upon the lamb, and so serve it up. Boil your lamb in a cloth.

Leg of Lamb, with forcemeat.

Slit a leg of lamb on the wrong side, and take out as much meat as possible, without cutting or cracking the outward skin. Pound this meat well with an equal weight of fresh suet: add to this the pulp of a dozen large oysters, and two anchovies boned and clean washed. Season the whole with salt, black-pepper, mace, a little thyme, parsley, and shalot, finely shred together; beat them all thoroughly with the yolks of three eggs, and, having filled the skin tight with this stuffing, sew it up very close. Tie it up to the spit and roast it. Serve it with any good sauce.

Shoulder of Lamb, grilled.

Half roast, then score, and season it with pepper, salt, and cayenne. Broil it; reserve the gravy carefully; pass it through a sieve to take off all fat. Mix with it mushroom and walnut ketchup, onion, the size of a nut, well bruised, a little chopped parsley, and some of the good jelly reserved for sauces. Put a good quantity of this sauce; make it boil, and pour it boiling hot on the lamb when sent to table.

Lamb, to ragout.

Roast a quarter of lamb, and when almost done dredge it well with grated bread, which must be put into the dish you serve it up in; take veal cullis, salt, pepper, anchovy, and lemon juice; warm it, lay the lamb in it, and serve it up.

Lamb, to fricassee.

Cut the hind quarter of lamb into thin slices, and season them with spice, sweet-herbs, and a shalot; fry and toss them up in some strong broth, with balls and palates, and a little brown gravy to thicken it.

Miscellaneous directions respecting Meat.

A leg of veal, the fillet without bone, the knuckle for steaks, and a pie; bone of fillet and knuckle for soup.—Shoulder of veal, knuckle cut off for soup.—Breast of veal, thin end stews, or re-heats as a stew.—Half a calf's head boils, then hashes, with gravy from the bones.—For mock turtle soup, neats' feet instead of calf's head, that is, two calves' feet and two neats' feet.—Giblets of all poultry make gravy.—Ox-cheek, for soup and kitchen. —Rump of beef cut in two, thin part roasted, thick boiled: or steaks and one joint, the bone for soup.—The trimmings of many joints will make gravy.— To boil the meat white, well flour the joint and the cloth it is boiled in, not letting any thing be boiled with it, and frequently skimming the grease.— Lamb chops fried dry and thin make a neat dish, with French beans in cream round them. A piece of veal larded in white celery sauce, to answer the chops.—Dressed meat, chopped fine, with a little forcemeat, and made into balls about the size of an egg, browned and fried dry, and sent up without any sauce.—Sweetbreads larded in white celery sauce.—To remove taint in meat, put the joint into a pot with water, and, when it begins to boil, throw in a few red clear cinders, let them boil together for two or three minutes, then take out the meat, and wipe it dry.—To keep hams, when they are cured for hanging up, tie them in brown paper bags tight round the hocks to exclude the flies, which omission occasions maggots.—Ginger, where spice is required, is very good in most things.

Meat, general rule for roasting and boiling.

The general rule for roasting and boiling meat is as follows: fifteen minutes to a pound in roasting, twenty minutes to a pound in boiling.

On no account whatever let the least drop of water be poured on any roast meat; it soddens it, and is a bad contrivance to make gravy, which is, after all, no gravy, and totally spoils the meat.

Meat, half-roasted or under-done.

Cut small pieces, of the size of a half-crown, of half-roasted mutton, and put them into a saucepan with half a pint of red wine, the same quantity of gravy, one anchovy, a little shalot, whole pepper, and salt; let them stew a little; then put in the meat with a few capers, and, when thoroughly hot, thicken with butter rolled in flour.

Mustard, to make.

Mix three table-spoonfuls of mustard, one of salt, and cold spring water sufficient to reduce it to a proper thickness.

Chine of Mutton, to roast.

Let the chine hang downward, and raise the skin from the bone. Take slices of lean gammon of bacon, and season it with chives, parsley, and white pepper; spread them over the chine, and lay the bacon upon them. Turn the skin over them, and tie it up; cover with paper, and roast. When nearly done, dredge with crumbs of bread, and serve up, garnishing with mutton cutlets.

Mutton chops, to stew.

Put them in a stewpan, with an onion, and enough cold water to cover them; when come to a boil, skim and set them over a very slow fire till tender; perhaps about three quarters of an hour.

Turnips may be boiled with them.

Mutton cutlets.

Cut a neck of mutton into cutlets; beat it till very tender; wash it with thick melted butter, and strew over the side which is buttered some sweet-herbs, chopped small, with grated bread, a little salt, and nutmeg. Lay it on a gridiron over a charcoal fire, and, turning it, do the same to that side as the other. Make sauce of gravy, anchovies, shalots, thick butter, a little nutmeg, and lemon.

Mutton cutlets, with onion sauce.

Cut the cutlets very small; trim all round, taking off all the fat; cut off the long part of the bone; put them into a stewpan, with all the trimmings that have been cut off, together with one onion cut in slices; add some parsley, a carrot or two, a pinch of salt, and six table-spoonfuls of mutton or veal jelly, and let them stew till the cutlets are of a brown colour all round, but do not let them burn. Take out the cutlets, drain them in a sieve, and let them cool; then strain the sauce till it becomes of a fine glaze, and re-warm them. Have ready some good onion sauce; put it in the middle of the dish; place the cutlets—eight, if they are small—round it, and serve the glaze with them; take care it does not touch the onion sauce, but pour it round the outside part.

Mutton hams, to make.

Cut a hind quarter of mutton like a ham. Take one ounce of saltpetre, one pound of coarse sugar, and one pound of common salt; mix them together, and rub the ham well with them. Lay it in a hollow tray with the skin downward; baste it every day for a fortnight; then roll it in sawdust, and hang it in wood smoke for a fortnight. Boil and hang it in a dry place; cut it out in rashers. It does not eat well boiled, but is delicious broiled.

Haricot Mutton.

Take a neck of mutton, and cut it in the same manner as for mutton chops. When done, lay them in your stewpan, with a blade of mace, some whole peppercorns, a bunch of sweet-herbs, two onions, one carrot, one turnip, all cut in slices, and lay them over your mutton. Set your stewpan over a slow fire, and let the chops stew till they are brown; turn them, that the other side may be the same. Have ready some good gravy, and pour on them, and let them stew till they are very tender. Your ragout must be turnips and carrots cut into dice, and small onions, all boiled very tender, and well stirred up in the liquor in which your mutton was stewed.

Another way.

Fry mutton chops in butter till they are brown, but not done through. Lay them flat in a stewpan, and just cover them with gravy. Put in small onions, whole carrots, and turnips, scooped or cut into shapes; let them stew very gently for two hours or more. Season the chops before you fry them with pepper and salt.

Leg of Mutton.

To give a leg of mutton the taste of mountain meat, hang it up as long as it will keep fresh; rub it every day with ginger and coarse brown sugar, leaving it on the meat.

Leg of Mutton in the French fashion.

A leg of mutton thus dressed is a very excellent dish. Pare off all the skin as neatly as possible; lard the leg with the best lard, and stick a few cloves here and there, with half a clove of garlic, laid in the shank. When half roasted, cut off three or four thin pieces, so as not to disfigure it, about the shank bone; mince these very fine with sage, thyme, mint, and any other sweet garden herbs; add a little beaten ginger, very little, three or four grains; as much cayenne pepper, two spoonfuls of lemon juice, two ladlefuls of claret wine, a few capers, the yolks of two hard-boiled eggs: stew these in some meat jelly, and, when thoroughly stewed, pour over your roast, and serve it up. Do not spare your meat jelly; let the sauce be in generous quantity.

Leg of Mutton or Beef, to hash.

Cut small flat pieces of the meat, taking care to pare the skin and sinews, but leaving as much fat as you can find in the inside of the leg; season with a little salt and cayenne pepper and a little soup jelly; put in two whole onions, two bunches of parsley, the same of thyme, and a table-spoonful of mushroom-powder. Take two or three little balls of flour and butter, of the size of a nut, to thicken the sauce; beat it well together; let this simmer a little while; take off the scum; put in the meat, and let it boil. Serve up hot, with fried bread round it.

Another way.

Take the mutton and cut it into slices, taking off the skin and fat; beat it well, and rub the dish with garlic; put in the mutton with water, and season with salt, an onion cut in half, and a bundle of savoury herbs; cover it, and set it over a stove and stew it. When half stewed, add a little white wine (say two glasses) three blades of mace, and an anchovy; stew it till enough done; then take out the onion and herbs, and put the hash into the dish, rubbing a piece of butter in flour to thicken it, and serve it up.

Loin of Mutton, to stew.

Cut your mutton in steaks, and put it into as much water as will cover it. When it is skimmed, add four onions sliced and four large turnips.

Neck of Mutton, to roast.

Draw the neck with parsley, and then roast it; and, when almost enough, dredge it with white pepper, salt, and crumbs; serve it with the juice of orange and gravy.

Neck of Mutton, to boil.

Lard a neck of mutton with lemon-peel, and then boil it in salt and water, with sweet-herbs. While boiling, stew a pint of oysters in their own liquor, half a pint of white wine, and the like quantity of broth; put in two or three whole onions and some anchovies, grated nutmeg, and a little thyme.

Thicken the broth with the yolks of four eggs, and dish it up with sippets. Lay the oysters under the meat, and garnish with barberries and lemon.

Neck of Mutton, to fry.

Take the best end of a neck of mutton, cut it into steaks, beat them with a rolling-pin, strew some salt on them, and lay them in a frying-pan: hold the pan over a slow fire that may not burn them: turn them as they heat, and there will be gravy enough to fry them in, till they are half done. Then put to them some good gravy; let them fry together, till they are done; add a good bit of butter, shake it up, and serve it hot with pickles.

Saddle of Mutton and Kidneys.

Raise the skin of the fore-chine of mutton, and draw it with lemon and thyme; and with sausage-meat farce part of it. Take twelve kidneys, farce, skewer, and afterwards broil them; and lay round horseradish between, with the gravy under.

Shoulder of Mutton, to roast in blood.

Cut the shoulder as you would venison; take off the skin, and let it lie in blood all night. Take as much powder of sweet-herbs as will lie on a sixpence, a little grated bread, pepper, nutmeg, ginger, and lemon-peel, the yolks of two eggs boiled hard, about twenty oysters, and some salt; temper these all together with the blood; stuff the meat thickly with it, and lay some of it about the mutton; then wrap the caul of the sheep about the shoulder; roast it, and baste it with blood till it is nearly done. Take off the caul, dredge, baste it with butter, and serve it with venison sauce. If you do not cut it venison fashion, yet take off the skin, because it will eat tough; let the caul be spread while it is warm, and, when you are to dress it, wrap it up in a cloth dipped in hot water. For sauce, take some of the bones of the breast; chop and put to them a whole onion, a little lemon-peel, anchovies, and a little spice. Stew these; add some red wine, oysters, and mushrooms.

Shoulder, or Leg of Mutton, with Oysters.

Make six holes in either a shoulder or leg of mutton with a knife: roll in eggs with your oysters, with crumbs and nutmeg, and stuff three or four in every hole. If you roast, put a caul over it; if for boiling, a napkin. Make some good oyster sauce, which lay under, and serve up hot.

Roasted Mutton, with stewed Cucumbers.

Bone a neck and loin of mutton, leaving on only the top bones, about an inch long; draw the one with parsley, and lard the other with bacon very closely; and, after skewering, roast them. Fry and stew your cucumbers; lay them under the mutton, and season them with salt, pepper, vinegar, and minced shalot, and put the sauce under the mutton, garnishing with pickled cucumbers and horseradish.

Mutton to eat like Venison.

Boil and skin a loin of mutton; take the bones, two onions, two anchovies, a bunch of sweet-herbs, some pepper, mace, carrot, and crust of bread; stew these all together for gravy; strain it off, and put the mutton into a stewpan with the fat side downward; add half a pint of port wine. Stew it till thoroughly done.

Mutton in epigram.

Roast a shoulder of mutton till it is three parts done, and let it cool; raise the skin quite up to the knuckle, and cut off all to the knuckle. Sauce the blade-bone; broil it, and hash the rest, putting in some capers, with good gravy, pickled cucumbers, and shalots. Stir them well up, and lay the blade-bone on the skin.

Mushrooms, to stew brown.

Take some pepper and salt, with a little cayenne and a little cream; thicken with butter and flour. To do them white, cut out all the black inside.

Newmarket John.

Cut the lean part of a leg of mutton in little thin collops; beat them; butter a stewpan, and lay the collops all over. Have ready pepper, salt, shalot or garlic, and strew upon them. Set them over a very slow fire. As the gravy draws, turn over the collops, and dredge in a very little flour; have ready some good hot gravy. Shake it up all together, and serve with pickles.

Ox-cheek, to stew.

Choose one that is fat and young, which may be known by the teeth; pick out the eye-balls; cut away the snout and all superfluous bits. Wash and clean it perfectly; well dry it in a cloth, and, with the back of a cleaver, break all the bones in the inside of the cheek; then with a rollingpin beat the flesh of the outside. If it is intended for the next day's dinner, proceed in this manner:—quarter and lard it with marrow; then pour on it garlic or elder vinegar so gently that it may sink into the flesh; strew salt over it, and let it remain so till morning. Then put it into a stewpan, big enough, if you do both cheeks, to admit of their lying flat close to one another; but first rub the pan well with garlic, and with a spoon spread a pound of butter and upwards at the bottom and sides of the pan. Strew cloves and beaten mace on the cheeks, also thyme and sweet marjoram, finely chopped; then put in as much white wine as will cover them an inch or more above the meat, but wash not off the other things by pouring it on. Rub the lid of the pan with garlic, and cover it so close that no steam can escape. Make a brisk fire under it, and, when the cover is so hot that you cannot bear your hand on it, then a slack fire will stew it, but keep it so that the cover be of the same heat as long as it is stewing. It must not be uncovered the whole time it is doing: about three hours will be sufficient. When you take it up, be careful not to break it; take out the loose bones; pour the liquor on the cheek; clear from the fat and the dross, and put lemon-juice to it. Serve it hot.

Another way.

Soak it in water, and make it very clean; put it in a gallon of water, with some potherbs, salt, and whole pepper. When stewed, so that the bones will slip out easily, take it up and strain off the soup; put a bit of butter in the frying-pan with some flour, and fry the meat brown, taking care not to burn it. Put some of the soup to the flour and butter, with ketchup, mushrooms, anchovy, and walnut liquor. Lay the cheek in a deep dish, and pour the sauce over it.

Ox-tail ragout.

Some good gravy must first be made, and the tail chopped through every joint, and stewed a long time in it till quite tender, with an onion stuck with cloves, a table-spoonful of port or Madeira wine, a tea-spoonful of soy, and a little cayenne. Thicken the gravy with a little flour.

Another.

Take two or three ox-tails; put them in a saucepan, with turnips, carrots, onions, and some black peppercorns; stew them for four hours. Take them out; cut them in pieces at every joint; put them into a stewpan with some good gravy, and scraped turnip and carrot; or cut them into the shape of a ninepin; pepper and salt to your taste; add the juice of half a lemon; and send it to table very hot.

Peas, to stew.

Take a quart of fine peas, and two small or one large cabbage lettuce; boil the lettuce tender; take it out of the water, shake it well, and put it into the stewpan, with about two ounces of butter, three or four little onions cut small, and the peas. Set them on a very slow fire, and let them stew about two hours; season them to your taste with pepper and a tea-spoonful of sugar; and, instead of salt, stew in some bits of ham, which you may take out or leave in when you serve it. There should not be a drop of water, except what inevitably comes from the lettuce.

Another way.

To your peas, add cabbage lettuces cut small, a small faggot of mint, and one onion; pass them over the fire with a small bit of butter, and, when they are tender and the liquor from them reduced, take out the onion and mint, and add a little white sauce. Take care it be not too thin; season with a little pepper and salt.

Green Peas, to keep till Christmas.

Gather your peas, when neither very young nor old, on a fine dry day. Shell, and let two persons holding a cloth, one at each end, shake them backward and forward for a few minutes. Put them into clean quart bottles; fill the bottles, and cork tight. Melt some rosin in a pipkin, dip the necks of the bottles into it, and set them in a cool dry place.

Another way.

Shell the peas, and dry them in a gentle heat, not much greater than that of a hot summer's day. Put them when quite dry into linen bags, and hang them up in a dry place. Before they are boiled, at Christmas or later, steep them in half milk, half water, for twelve or fourteen hours; then boil them as if fresh gathered. Beans and French beans may be preserved in the same manner.

Red Pickle, for any meat.

A quarter of a pound of saltpetre, a large common basinful of coarse sugar, and coarse salt. A leg of pork to lie in it a fortnight.

Beef Steak Pie.

Rump steaks are preferable to beef; season them with the usual seasoning, puff-paste top and bottom, and good gravy to fill the dish.

Calf's Head Pie.

Parboil the head; cut it into thin slices; season with pepper and salt; lay them into a crust with some good gravy, forcemeat balls, and yolks of eggs boiled hard. Bake it about an hour and a half; cut off the lid; thicken some good gravy with a little flour; add some oysters; serve it with or without a lid.

Mutton or Grass Lamb Pie.

Take a loin of mutton or lamb, and clear it from fat and skin; cut it into steaks; season them well with pepper and salt; almost fill the dish with water; lay puff paste at top and bottom.

Veal Pie (common).

Make exactly as you would a beef-steak pie.

Veal Pie (rich).

Take a neck, a fillet, or a breast of veal, cut from it your steaks, seasoned with pepper, salt, nutmeg, and a few cloves, truffles, and morels; then slice two sweetbreads; season them in the same manner, and put a layer of paste round the dish; then lay the meat, yolks of eggs boiled hard, and oysters at the top: fill it with water. When taken out of the oven, pour in at the top through a funnel some good boiled gravy, thickened with cream and flour boiled up.

Veal and Ham Pie.

Take two pounds of veal cutlets, or the best end of the neck, cut them in pieces about half the size of your hand, seasoned with pepper and a very little salt, and some dressed ham in slices. Lay them alternately in the dish with forcemeat or sausage meat, the yolks of three eggs boiled hard, and a gill of water.

Veal Olive Pie.

Make your olives as directed in the receipt for making olives; put them into a crust; fill the pie with water: when baked, pour in some good gravy, boiled and thickened with a little good cream and flour boiled together. These ingredients make an excellent pie.

Beef Olive Pie.

Make your olives as you would common beef olives; put them into puff paste, top and bottom; fill the pie with water, when baked, pour in some good rich gravy.

Pig, to barbicue.

The best pig for this purpose is of the thick neck breed, about six weeks old. Season the barbicue very high with cayenne, black pepper, and sage, finely sifted; which must be rubbed well into the inside of the pig. It must then be sewed up and roasted, or, if an oven can be depended upon, it will be equally good baked. The sauce must be a very high beef gravy, with an equal quantity of Madeira wine in it. Send the pig to table whole. Be careful not to put any salt into the pig, as it will change its colour.

Pig, to collar.

Have your pig cut down the back, and bone and wash it clean from the blood; dry it well, and season it with spice, salt, parsley, and thyme, and roll it hard in a collar; tie it close in a dry cloth and boil it with the bones, in three pints of water, a quart of vinegar, a handful of salt, a faggot of sweet-herbs, and whole spice. When tender, let it cool and take it off; take it out of the cloth, and keep it in the pickle.

Pig, to collar in colours.

Boil and wash your pig well, and lay it on a dresser: chop parsley, thyme, and sage, and strew them over the inside of the pig. Beat some mace and cloves, mix with them some pepper and salt, and strew that over. Boil some eggs hard, chop the yolks, and put them in layers across your pig; boil some beet-root, and cut that into slices, and lay them across; then roll it up in a cloth and boil it. Before it is cold, press it with a weight, and it will be fit for use.

Pig, to pickle or souse.

Take a fair fat pig, cut off his head, and cut him through the middle. Take out the brains, lay them in warm water, and leave them all night. Roll the pig up like brawn, boil till tender, and then throw it into an earthen pan with salt and water. This will whiten and season the flesh; for no salt must be put into the boiling for fear of turning it black. Then take a quart of this broth and a quart of white wine, boil them together, and put in three or four bay-leaves: when cold, season your pig, and put it into this sauce. It will keep three months.

Pig, to roast.

Chop the liver small by itself: mince blanched bacon, capers, truffles, anchovy, mushrooms, sweet-herbs and garlic. Season and blanch the whole. Fill your pig with it; tie it up; sprinkle some good olive oil over it; roast and serve it up hot.

Another way.

Put a piece of bread, parsley, and sage, cut small, into the belly with a little salt; sew up the belly; spit the pig, and roast it; cut off the ears and the under-jaws, which you will lay round; making a sauce with the brains, thick butter and gravy, which lay underneath.

Pig, to dress lamb fashion.

After skinning the pig, but leaving the skin quite whole, with the head on, chine it down, as you would do mutton, larding it with thyme and lemon-peel; and roast it in quarters like lamb. Fill the other part with a plum-pudding; sew the belly up, and bake it.

Pigs' Feet and Ears, fricassee of.

Clean the feet and ears, and boil them very tender. Cut them in small shreds, the length of a finger and about a quarter of an inch in breadth; fry them in butter till they are brown but not hard; put them into a stewpan with a little brown gravy and a good piece of butter, two spoonfuls of vinegar, and a good deal of mustard—enough to flavour it strong. Salt to your taste; thicken with very little flour. Put in half an onion; then take the feet, which should likewise be boiled as tender as for eating; slit them quite through the middle; take out the large bones; dip them in eggs, and strew them over with bread crumbs, seasoned with pepper and salt; boil or fry them, and put them on the ragout, into which squeeze some lemon-juice.

Pigs' Feet and Ears, ragout of.

Split the feet, and take them out of souse; dip them in eggs, then in bread-crumbs and chopped parsley; fry them in lard. Drain them; cut the ears in long narrow slips; flour them; put them into some good gravy; add ketchup, morels, and pickled mushrooms; stew them into the dish, and lay on the feet.

Pig's Head, to roll.

Take the belly-piece and head of pork, rub it well with saltpetre and a very little salt; let it lie three or four days; wash it clean; then boil the head tender, and take off all the meat with the ears, which cut in pieces. Have ready four neats' feet, also well boiled; take out the bones, cut the meat in thin slices, mix it with the head, and lay it with the belly-piece: roll it up tight, and bind it up, and set it on one end, with a trencher upon it; set it within the tin, and place a heavy weight upon that, and let it stand all night. In the morning take it out, and bind it with a fillet; put it in some salt and water, which must be changed every four or five days. When sliced, it looks like brawn. It is also good dipped in butter and fried, and eaten with melted butter, mustard, and vinegar: for that purpose the slices should be only about three inches square.

Pilaw, an Indian dish.

Take six or eight ribs of a neck of mutton; separate and take off all the skin and fat, and put them into a stewpan with twelve cloves, a small piece of ginger, twelve grains of black pepper, and a little cinnamon and mace, with one clove of garlic. Add as much water as will serve to stew these ingredients thoroughly and make the meat tender. Then take out the mutton, and fry it in nice butter of a light brown, with some small onions chopped fine and fried very dry; put them to the mutton-gravy and spice in which it was stewed, adding a table-spoonful of curry-powder and half an ounce of butter. After mixing all the above ingredients well together, put them to the rice, which should be previously half boiled, and let the whole stew together, until the rice is done enough and the gravy completely absorbed. When the pilaw is dished for table, it should be thinly covered with plain boiled rice to make it look white, and served up very hot.

Pork, to collar.

Bone and season a breast of pork with savoury spice, parsley, sage, and thyme; roll it in a hard collar of cloth; tie it close, and boil it, and, when cold, keep it in souse.

Pork, to pickle.

Having boned your pork, cut it into such pieces as will lie most conveniently to be powdered. The tub used for this purpose must be sufficiently large and sound, so as to hold the brine; and the narrower and deeper it is the better it will keep the meat. Well rub the meat with saltpetre; then take one part of bay and two parts of common salt, and rub every piece well, covering it with salt, as you would a flitch of bacon. Strew salt in the bottom of the tub; lay the pieces in it as closely as possible, strewing salt round the sides of the tub, and if the salt should even melt at the top strew no more. Meat thus cured will keep a long time.

Another way.

Cut your pork into small pieces, of the size you would boil at one time; rub all the pieces very well with salt, and lay them on a dresser upon boards made to slope that the brine may run off. After remaining three or four days, wipe them with a dry cloth; have ready a quantity of salt mixed with a small portion of saltpetre: rub each piece well with this mixture, after which cover them all over with salt. Put them into an earthen jar, or large pan, placing the pieces as close together as possible, closing the top of the jar or pan, so as to prevent all external air from getting in; put the shoulder pieces in a pan by themselves. Pork prepared in this manner will keep good a year.

Chine of Pork, to stuff and roast.

Make your stuffing of parsley, sage, thyme, eggs, crumbs of bread, and season it with salt, pepper, nutmeg, and shalot; stuff the chine thick, and roast it gently. When about a quarter roasted, cut the skin in slips, making your sauce with lemon-peel, apples, sugar, butter, and mustard, just as you would for a roast leg.

Another way.

Take a chine of pork that has hung four or five days; make holes in the lean, and stuff it with a little of the fat leaf, chopped very small, some parsley, thyme, a little sage, and shalot, cut very fine, and seasoned with pepper and salt. It should be stuffed pretty thick. Have some good gravy in the dish. For sauce, use apple sauce.

Pork Cutlets.

Cut off the skin of a loin or neck of pork and make cutlets; season them with parsley, sage, and thyme, mixed together with crumbs of bread, pepper, and salt; broil them, and make sauce with mustard, butter, shalot, and gravy, and serve up hot.

Gammon, to roast.

Let the gammon soak for twenty-four hours in warm water. Boil it tender, but not too much. When hot, score it with your knife; put some pepper on it, and then put it into a dish to crisp in a hot oven; but be mindful to pull the skin off.

Leg of Pork, to broil.

After skinning part of the fillet, cut it into slices, and hack it with the back of your knife; season with pepper, salt, thyme, and sage, minced small. Broil the slices on the gridiron, and serve with sauce made with drawn butter, sugar, and mustard.

Spring of Pork, to roast.

Cut off the spring of a knuckle of pork, and leave as much skin on the spring as you can, parting it from the neck, and taking out the bones. Rub it well with salt, and strew it all over with thyme shred small, parsley, sage, a nutmeg, cloves, and mace, beaten small and well mixed together. Rub all well in, and roll the whole up tight, with the flesh inward. Sew it fast, spit it lengthwise, and roast it.

Potatoes, to boil. No. 1.

The following is the celebrated Lancashire receipt for cooking potatoes:—Cleanse them well, put them in cold water, and boil them with their skins on exceedingly slow. When the water bubbles, throw in a little cold water. When they are done, drain the water completely away through a colander; return them into a pot or saucepan without water; cover them up, and set them before the fire for a quarter of an hour longer. Do not pare the potatoes before they are boiled, which is a very unwholesome and wasteful practice.

Potatoes, to boil. No. 2.

Scrape off the rind; put them into an iron pot; simmer them till they begin to crack, and allow a fork to pierce easily; then pour off the water, and put aside the lid of the pot, and sprinkle over some salt. Place your pot at the edge of the fire, and there let it remain an hour or more, and during this time all the moisture of the potatoes will gradually exhale in steam, and you will find them white or flaky as snow. Take them out with a spoon or ladle.

Potatoes, to boil. No. 3.

Boil them as usual; half an hour before sending to table, throw away the water from them, and set the pot again on the fire; sufficient moisture will come from the potatoes to prevent the pot from burning; let them stand on the half stove, and not be peeled until sent to table.

Potatoes, to bake.

Wash nicely, make into balls, and bake in the Dutch oven a light brown. This forms a neat side or corner dish.

Potato balls.

Pound some boiled potatoes in a mortar, with the yolks of two eggs, a little pepper, and salt; make them in balls about the size of an egg; do them over with yolk of egg and crumbs of bread; then fry them of a light brown for table; five balls for a corner dish.

Croquets of Potatoes.

Boil some potatoes in water, strain them, and take sufficient milk to make them into a mash, rather thick; before you mix the potatoes put the peel of half a lemon, finely grated, one lump of sugar, and a pinch of salt; strain the milk after heating it, and add the potatoes; mash them well together; let the mash cool; roll it into balls of the shape and size of an egg; let there be ten or twelve of them; brush them over with the yolk of egg, and roll them in crumbs of bread and a pinch of salt. Do this twice over; then fry them of a fine brown colour, and serve them with fried parsley round.

Potatoes, to fry.

After your potatoes are nicely boiled and skinned, grate them, and to every large table-spoonful of potatoes add one egg well beat, and to each egg a small spoonful of cream, with some salt. Drop as many spoonfuls as are proper in a pan in which is clarified butter.

Potatoes, to mash.

After the potatoes are boiled and peeled, mash them in a mortar, or on a clean board, with a broad knife, and put them into a stewpan. To two pounds of potatoes put in half a pint of milk, a quarter of a pound of butter, and a little salt; set them over the fire, and keep them stirred till the butter is melted; but take care they do not burn to the bottom. Dish them up in what form you please.

Potatoes, French way of cooking.

Boil the potatoes in a weak white gravy till nearly done; stir in some cream and vermicelli, with three or four blades of mace, and let it boil till the potatoes are sufficiently done, without being broken.

Potatoes, à-la-Maitre d'hotel.

Cut boiled potatoes into slices, not too thin; simmer them in a little plain gravy, a bit of butter rubbed in a little flour, chopped parsley, pepper, and salt, and serve hot.

Rice, to boil.

To boil rice well, though a simple thing, is rarely well done. Have two quarts of water boiling, while you wash six ounces of rice, picked clean. Change the water three or four times. When the rice is clean, drain and put it into the boiling water. Boil twenty minutes; add three quarters of a tablespoonful of salt. Drain off the water well—this is the most essential point—set it before the fire, spread thin to dry. When dry, serve it up. If the rice is not dry, so that each grain separates easily from the others, it is not properly boiled.

Another way.

Put one pound of rice into three quarts of boiling water; let it remain twenty minutes. Skim the water, and add one ounce of hog's lard and a little salt and pepper. Let it simmer gently over the fire closely covered, for an hour and a quarter, when it will be fit for use. This will produce eight pounds of savoury rice.

Rissoles. No. 1.

Take a roasted fowl, turkey, or pullet; pull it into shreds; there must be neither bone nor skin. Cut some veal and ham into large dice; put it into a stewpan, with a little thyme, carrots, onions, cloves, and two or three mushrooms. Make these ingredients simmer over a slow fire for two hours, taking care they do not burn; put in a handful of flour, and stir well, with a pint of cream and as much good broth; let the whole then stew for a quarter of an hour; continue to stir with a wooden spoon to prevent its burning. When it is done enough, strain it through a woollen strainer; then put in the whole meat of the poultry you have cut, with which you must make little balls of the size of pigeons' eggs. Dip them twice in very fine crumbs of bread; wrap them in paste, rolled very thin; then fry them in lard, which should be very hot.

Rissoles. No. 2.

Take the fleshy parts and breasts of two fowls, which cut into small dice, all of an equal size; then throw them into some white sauce, and reduce it till it becomes very thick and stiff. When this is cold, cut it into several pieces, and roll them to the size and shape of a cork; then roll them in crumbs of bread very fine; dip them into some white and yolks of eggs put up together with a little salt, and roll them again in bread. If they are not stiff enough to keep their shape, this must be repeated; then fry them of a light brown colour, drain them, wipe off the grease, and serve them with fried parsley between them.

Rissoles. No. 3.

Take of the puré made as directed for pheasant, veal, or game, (see Pheasant under the head Game) a sufficient quantity for eight rissoles, then a little of the jelly of veal, say about half a pint; put in it a pinch of salt and of cayenne pepper, two table-spoonfuls of cream, the yolk of one egg, and a piece of butter of the size of a walnut; mix this sauce well together over the fire, strain it, and then add the puré. Let it cool, and prepare a little puff-paste sufficient to wrap the rissoles once over with it, taking care to roll the paste out thin. Fry them, and send them up with fried parsley, without sauce. The rissoles must be made stiff enough not to break in the frying.

Rice.

One pound of veal or fowl, chopped fine; have ready some good bechamel sauce mixed with parsley and lemon-juice; mix it of a good thickness. When cold, make it up into balls, or what shape you please; dip them in yolks of eggs and bread crumbs, and fry them a few minutes before they go to table. They should be of a light brown, and sent up with fried parsley.

A Robinson, to make.

Take about eight or ten pounds of the middle of a brisket of beef; let it hang a day; then salt it for three days hung up; afterwards put it in strong red pickle, in which let it remain three weeks. Take it out, put it into a pot with plenty of water, pepper, a little allspice, and onion; let it simmer for seven or eight hours, but never let it boil. When quite tender, take out all the bones, spread it out on a table to cool, well beat it out with a rollingpin, and sprinkle with cayenne, nutmeg, and very little cloves, pounded together. Put it in a coarse cloth after it is rolled; twist it at each end to get out the fat, and bind it well round with broad tape; in that state let it remain three days.

Salad, to dress.

Two or three eggs, two or three anchovies, pounded, a little tarragon chopped very fine, a little thick cream, mustard, salt, and cayenne pepper, mixed well together. After these are all well mixed, add oil, a little tarragon, elder, and garlic vinegar, so as to have the flavour of each, and then a little of the French vinegar, if there is not enough of the others to give the requisite taste.

Bologna Sausages.

Have the fillets of young, tender porkers, and out of the weight of twenty-five pounds three parts are to be lean and one fat; season them well in the small shredding with salt and pepper, a little grated nutmeg, and a pint of white wine, mixed with a pint of hog's blood; stirring and beating it well together, with a little of the sweet-herbs finely chopped; with a funnel open the mouths of the guts, and thrust the meat gently into it with a clean napkin, as by forcing it with your hands you may break the gut. Divide them into what lengths you please; tie them with fine thread, and let them dry in the air for two or three days, if the weather be clear and a brisk wind, hanging them in rows at a little distance from each other in the smoke-loft. When well dried, rub off the dust they contract with a clean cloth; pour over them sweet olive-oil, and cover them with a dry earthen vessel.

English Sausages.

Chop and bruise small the lean of a fillet of young pork; to every pound put a quarter of a pound of fat, well skinned, and season it with a little nutmeg, salt, and pepper, adding a little grated bread; mix all these well together, and put it into guts, seasoned with salt and water.

Another way.

Take six pounds of very fine well fed pork, quite free from gristle and fat; cut it very small, and beat it fine in a mortar; shred six pounds of suet, free from skin, as fine as possible. Take a good deal of sage, the leaves picked off and washed clean, and shred fine as possible; spread the meat on a clean table; then shake the sage, about three large spoonfuls, all over; shred the yellow part of the rind of a lemon very fine, and throw that over, with as much sweet-herbs, when shred fine, as will fill a large spoon; grate two nutmegs over it, with two tea-spoonfuls of bruised pepper, and a large spoonful of salt. Then throw over it the suet, and mix all well together, and put it down close in a pot. When you use it, roll it up with as much beaten egg as will make the sausages roll smooth; let what you fry them in be hot before you put them into the pan; roll them about, and when they are thoroughly hot, and of a fine light brown colour, they are done. By warming a little of the meat in a spoon when you are making it, you will then taste if it is seasoned enough.

Sausages for Scotch collops.

Take beef suet and some veal, with a little winter savory, sage, thyme, and some grated nutmeg, beaten cloves, mace, and a little salt and pepper. Let these be well beaten together; then add two eggs beat, and heat all together. Roll them up in grated bread, fry, and send them up.

Veal Sausages.

Take half a pound of the lean of a leg of veal; cut it in small pieces, and beat it very fine in a stone mortar, picking out all the little strings. Shred one pound and half of beef-suet very small; season it with pepper, salt, cloves, and mace, but twice as much mace as cloves, some sage, thyme, and sweet marjoram, according to your palate. Mix all these well with the yolks of twelve eggs; roll them to your fancy, and fry them in lard.

Sausages without skins.

Take a pound and quarter of the lean of a leg of veal and a pound and quarter of the lean of a hind loin of pork; pick the meat from the skins before you weigh it; then take two pounds and half of fresh beef-suet picked clean from the skins, and an ounce and half of red sage leaves, picked from the stalks; wash and mince them as fine as possible; put them to the meat and suet, and mince as fine as you can. Add to it two ounces of white salt and half an ounce of pepper. Pare all the crust from a stale penny French roll, and soak the crumb in water till it is wet through; put it into a clean napkin, and squeeze out all the water. Put the bread to the meat, with four new-laid eggs beaten; then with your hands work all these things together, and put them into a clean earthen pan, pressed down close. They will keep good for a week. When you use this meat, divide a pound into eighteen parts; flour your hands a little, and roll it up into pretty thick sausages, and fry them in sweet butter; a little frying will do.

Spinach, the best mode of dressing.

Boil the spinach, squeeze the water from it completely, chop it a little; then put it and a piece of butter in a stewpan with salt and a very little nutmeg; turn it over a brisk fire to dry the remaining water. Then add a little flour; mix it well, wet it with a little good broth, and let it simmer for some time, turning it now and then to prevent burning.

To dress it *maigre*, put cream instead of broth, and an onion with a clove stuck in it, which you take out when you serve the spinach. Garnish with fried bread. Observe that if you leave water in it, the spinach cannot ever be good.

Another way.

Clean it well, and throw it into fresh water; then squeeze and drain it quite dry. Chop it extremely small, and put it into a pan with cream, fresh butter, salt, and a very small quantity of pepper and nutmeg: add an onion with two cloves stuck in it, and serve it up very hot, with fried bread sippets of triangular shape round the dish.

Spinach, to stew.

Pick the spinach very carefully; put it into a pan of water; boil it in a large vessel with a good deal of salt to preserve the green colour, and press it down frequently that it may be done equally. When boiled enough to squeeze easily, drain it from the water, and throw it into cold water. When quite cold, make it into balls, and squeeze it well. Then spread it on a table and chop it very fine; put a good piece of butter in a stewpan, and lay the spinach over the butter. Let it dry over a slow fire, and add a little flour; moisten with half a pint of beef jelly and a very little warm water: add a little cayenne pepper. This spinach should be very like thick melted butter, and as fine and smooth as possible.

Another way.

Take some fine spinach, pick and wash it extremely clean. When well boiled, put it into cold water, and squeeze it in a cloth very dry; chop it very small; put it in a stewpan with a piece of butter and half a pint of good cream; stir it well over the fire, that it may not oil; and put in a little more cream just as you are going to dish it.

Sweetbreads, ragout of.

Wash your sweetbreads; put them into boiling water, and, after blanching them, throw them into cold water; dry them with a linen cloth; and put them in a saucepan over the fire with salt, pepper, melted bacon, and a faggot of sweet-herbs. Shake them together, and put some good gravy to moisten them; simmer over the fire, and thicken to your liking.

Another.

Take sweetbreads and lamb's fry, and parboil them, cutting them into slices, and cocks'-combs sliced and blanched, and season them with pepper and salt, and other spices; fry them in a little lard; drain and toss them in good gravy, with two shalots, a bunch of sweet-herbs, mushrooms, and truffles. Thicken it with a glass of claret; garnish with red beet root.

Savoury Toasts, to relish Wine.

Cut six or seven pieces of bread about the size of two fingers, and fry them in butter till they are of a good colour; cut as many slices of ham of the same size, and put them into a stewpan over a slow fire, for an hour; when they are done take them out, and stir into the stewpan a little flour; when of a good colour moisten it with some broth, without salt; then skim off the fat, and strain the sauce through a sieve. Dish the ham upon the fried bread, and pour the sauce over.

Another_Savoury_Toasts_to_relish_Wine.

Rasp some crumb of bread; put it over the fire in butter; put over it a minced veal kidney, with its fat, parsley, scallions, a shalot, cayenne pepper and salt, mixed with the whites and yolks of four eggs beat: put this forcemeat on fried toasts of bread, covering the whole with grated bread, and passing the salamander over it. Serve it with a clear beef gravy sauce under it.

Tomata to eat with roast meat.

Cover the bottom of a flat saucepan with the tomatas, that they may lie one upon another; add two or three spoonfuls of water, a little salt and pepper, to your taste; cover the pan, and stew them; in six or seven minutes turn them, and let them stew till they are soft. Send them up with their liquor.

Tongues, to cure. No. 1.

Take two fine bullocks' tongues; wash them well in spring water; dry them thoroughly with a cloth, and salt them with common salt, a quarter of a pound of saltpetre, a quarter of a pound of treacle, and a quarter of a pound of gunpowder. Let them lie in this pickle for a month; turn and rub them every day; then take them out and dry them with a cloth; rub a little gunpowder over them, and hang them up for a month, when they will be fit to eat, previously soaking a few hours as customary.

Tongues, to cure. No. 2.

One pound of bay salt, half a pound of saltpetre, two ounces of sal prunella, two pounds of coarse sugar; make your brine strong enough with common salt to float an egg. The quantity of water is seven quarts, boil all together, and scum it well for half an hour. When cold, put the tongues in, and wash them in warm water before dressing. For table be sure never to let them boil, but simmer slowly for four or five hours.

Tongues, to cure. No. 3.

Take two fine neats' tongues; cut off the roots, and cut a nick in the under side; wash them clean, and dry with a cloth. Rub them with common salt, and lay them on a board all night. Next day take two ounces of bay salt, one of sal prunella, and a handful of juniper-berries, all bruised fine; mix them with a quarter of a pound of coarse sugar and one pound of common salt. Rub the tongues well with this mixture; lay them in a long pan, and turn and rub them daily for a fortnight. Take them out of the pickle, and either dry or dress them.

Tongues, to cure. No. 4.

Mix some well bruised bay salt, and a little saltpetre, with common salt, and with a linen cloth rub the tongues and salt them, most particularly the roots; and as the brine consumes put some more, till the tongues are hard and stiff. When they are salted, roll them up, and dry them in bran.

Tongues, to cure. No. 5.

Have the roots well cleansed from the moisture, and with warm water wash and open the porous parts, that the salt may penetrate, and dry them well. Cover them for a week with a pickle made of common salt, and bay salt well boiled in it; then rub them with saltpetre, and to make them of a good red colour you must take them out, and rub and salt them well so that the salt penetrates, pressing them down hard with a board that, when they are put to dry, they may keep their due proportion. The usual way of drying them is with burnt sawdust, which, with the salt, gives the dusky colour that appears on the outside before they are boiled.

Tongues, to cure. No. 6.

Well rub into the tongue two ounces of saltpetre, a pound of common salt, and a quarter of a pound of treacle; and baste every day for three weeks.

Tongue, to smoke.

Wipe the tongue dry, when taken out of the pickle; glaze it over with a brush dipped in pyroligneous acid, and hang it up in the kitchen.

Tongue, to bake.

Season your tongues with pepper, salt, and nutmeg; lard them with large lardoons, and have them steeped all night in vinegar, claret, and ginger. Season again with whole pepper, sliced nutmeg, whole cloves, and salt. Bake them in an earthen pan; serve them up on sippets, and lay your spice over them, with slices of lemon and some sausages.

Tongue, to boil.

Put a good quantity of hay with your tongues, tying them up in a cloth, or else in hay. Boil them till they are tender and of a good colour, and they will eat short and mellow.

Tongue, to pot.

Prick the tongues with a skewer, and salt them with bay-salt and saltpetre, to make them red. Boil them till they will just peel; season with mace and a little pepper, to your liking; bake them in a pot well covered with butter, and they will keep as long as any potted meat.

Tongue and Udder, to roast.

Have the tongue and udder boiled and blanched, the tongue being salted with saltpetre; lard them with the whole length of large lardoons, and then roast them on a spit, basting them with butter: when roasted, dress them with grated bread and flour, and serve up with gravy, currant-jelly by itself, and slices of lemon.

Sheep's Tongue, or any other, with Oysters.

Boil six tongues in salt and water till they are sufficiently tender to peel. Slice them thin, and with a quart of large oysters put them in a dish, with some whole spice and a little claret, and let them stew together. Then put in some butter, and three yolks of eggs well beaten. Shake them all well together, and put some sippets and lay your tongues upon them.

Tripe, to dress.

Take of the finest tripe, and, when properly trimmed, cut it in pieces about four inches square; put it in a stewpan, with as much white wine as will almost cover it: slice in three or four race of ginger, quarter in a nutmeg, put in a good deal of salt, a bundle of herbs, rosemary, thyme, sweet marjoram, and onion. When this has stewed gently a good while, take out a pint of the clearest liquor, free from fat or dross, and dissolve in it some anchovies finely picked. Take up the tripe, a bit at a time, with a fork, and lay it in a warmed dish; pour on it the liquor in which the anchovies were dissolved. Sprinkle on it a little lemon juice. Those who are fond of onions or garlic may make either the prevailing ingredient.

Tripe, to fricassee.

Cut into slices the fat part of double tripe; dip them into eggs or batter, and fry them to lay round the dish. Cut the other part into long slips, and into dice, and toss them up with onion, chopped parsley, melted butter, yolks of eggs, and a little vinegar. Season with pepper and salt, and serve up.

Truffles and Morels, to stew.

Well wash the truffles, cut them into slices, of the size and about the thickness of half-a-crown; put them into a stewpan, with a pinch of salt and cayenne pepper, and a little butter, to prevent their being burnt. Let them stew ten minutes; have ready a good brown sauce of half a pint of beef and the same of veal jelly, thickened with a little butter and flour; add to it any trimmings of the truffles or morels, and boil them also in it; put in one pinch of cayenne pepper. Strain the truffles or morels from the butter they were first stewed in; throw them into the sauce; warm the whole again, and serve hot.

Veal, to boil.

Veal should be boiled well; a knuckle of six pounds will take very nearly two hours. The neck must be also well boiled in a good deal of water; if boiled in a cloth, it will be whiter. Serve it with tongue, bacon, or pickled pork, greens of any sort, brocoli, and carrots, or onion sauce, white sauce, oyster sauce, parsley and butter, or white celery sauce.

Veal, to collar.

Bone and wash a breast of veal; steep it in three waters, and dry it with a cloth; season it with savoury spice, some slices of bacon, and shred sweet-herbs; roll them in a collar of cloth, and boil it in salt and water, with whole spice; skim it clean and take it up, and when cold put it in the pickle.

Another way.

Take the meat of a breast of veal; make a stuffing of beef-suet, crumb of bread, lemon peel, parsley, pepper, and salt, mixed up with two eggs; lay it over the meat, and roll it up. Boil an hour and a half, and send it to table with oyster sauce.

Veal, to roast.

Veal will take a quarter of an hour to a pound: paper the fat of the loin and fillet; stuff the fillet and shoulder with the following ingredients: a quarter of a pound of suet, chopped fine, parsley, and sweet-herbs chopped, grated bread, lemon-peel, pepper, salt, nutmeg, and yolk of egg; butter may supply the want of suet. Roast the breast with the caul on it till almost done; take it off, flour and baste it. Veal requires to be more done than beef. For sauce use salad pickles, brocoli, cucumbers, raw or stewed, French beans, peas, cauliflower, celery, raw or stewed.

Veal, roasted, ragout of.

Cut slices of veal about the size of two fingers and at least as long as three; beat them with a cleaver till they are no thicker than a crown-piece; put upon every slice some stuffing made with beef-suet, ham, a little thyme, parsley, scallions, and a shalot. When the whole is minced, add the yolks of two eggs, half a table-spoonful of brandy, salt, and pepper; spread it on the veal and roll it. Cover each piece with a thin slice of bacon, and tie it carefully. Then put them on a small delicate spit covered with paper; and, when they are done, take off the paper carefully, grate bread over them, and brown them at a clear fire. Serve them with a gravy sauce.

Veal, to stew.

Cut the veal into small pieces; season with an onion, some salt and pepper, mace, lemon-peel, and two or three shalots; let them stew in water, with a little butter, or port wine, if you like. When enough done, put in some yolks of eggs beaten, and boil them quick. Dish and serve them up.

Veal, with Rice, to stew.

Boil half a pound of rice in three quarts of water in a small pan with some good broth, about a pint, and slices of ham at the bottom, and two good onions. When it is almost done, spread it, about twice the thickness of a crown-piece, over a silver or delft dish in which it is to be served [it must be a dish capable of bearing the fire]. Lay slices of veal and ham alternately —the veal having already been dressed brown. Cover the meat with rice in such a manner that it cannot be seen; put your dish upon a hot stove; brown the rice with a salamander; drain off the fat that may be in the dish, and serve it dry, or, if it is preferred, with any of the good sauces, for which there are directions, poured under it.

Veal served in paper.

Cut some slices of veal from the fillet, about an inch thick, in a small square, about the size of a small fricandeau; make a box of paper to fit neatly; rub the outside with butter, and put in your meat, with sweet oil or butter, parsley, scallions, shalots, and mushrooms, all stewed very fine, salt, and whole pepper. Set it upon the gridiron, with a sheet of oiled paper under it, and let it do by a very slow fire, lest the paper burn. When the meat is done on one side turn it on the other. Serve it in the box, having put over it very gently a dash of vinegar.

Bombarded Veal.

Take a piece of a long square of bacon; cut it in thin slices; do the same with veal, and lay the slices on your bacon. Having made a piece of good forcemeat, spread it thin on your veal, having previously seasoned the latter with pepper and salt. Roll these up one by one; spit them on a lark spit, quite even; wash them over with eggs and crumbs of bread; then roast them, and serve up with a good ragout.

Veal Balls.

Take two pounds of veal; pick out the skin and bones; mix it well with the crust of a French roll, soaked in hot milk, half a pound of veal suet, two yolks of eggs, onion, and chopped parsley; season with pepper and salt. Roll the balls in raspings; fry them of a gold colour: boil the bones and the bits of skin to make the gravy for them.

Breast of Veal.

To fricassee it like fowls, parboil it; turn it a few times over the fire with a bit of butter, a bunch of parsley, scallions, some mushrooms, truffles, and morels. Shake in a little flour; moisten with some good stock broth; and when the whole is done and skimmed, thicken it with the yolks of three eggs beat with some milk; and, before it is served, add a very little lemon juice.

Breast of Veal, with Cabbage and Bacon.

Cut the breast of veal in pieces, and parboil it; parboil also a cabbage and a bit of streaked bacon, cut in slices, leaving the rind to it. Tie each separately with packthread, and let them stew together with good broth; no salt or pepper, on account of the bacon. When the whole is done, take out the meat and cabbage, and put them into the terrine you serve to table. Take the fat off the broth, put in a little cullis, and reduce the sauce over the stove. When of a proper thickness pour it over the meat, and serve up.

Breast of Veal en fricandeau.

Lard your veal, and take a ragout of asparagus, (for which see Ragouts,) and lay your veal, larded or glazed, upon the ragout. The same may be done with a ragout of peas.

Breast of Veal, glazed brown.

Take a breast of veal, cut in pieces, or whole if you prefer it. Stir a bit of butter and a spoonful of flour over the fire, and, when it is of a good colour, put in a pint of broth, and afterwards the veal. Stew it over a slow fire, and season with pepper and salt, a bunch of parsley, scallions, cloves, thyme, laurel, basil, and half a spoonful of vinegar. When the meat is done and well glazed, skim the sauce well, and serve it round it.

Breast of Veal, to stew with Peas.

Cut the nicest part of the breast of veal, with the sweetbread; roast it a little brown; take a little bit of the meat that is cut off the ends, and fry it with butter, salt, pepper, and flour; take a little hot water just to rinse out the gravy that adheres to the frying-pan, and put it into a stewpan, with two quarts of hot water, a bundle of parsley, thyme, and marjoram, a bit of onion or shalot, plenty of lemon-peel, and a pint of old green peas, the more mealy the better. Let it stew two or three hours, then rub it through a sieve with a spoon; it should be all nice and thick; then put it again in the stewpan with the meat, having ready some hot water to add to the gravy in case it should be wanted. A thick breast will take two hours, and must be turned every now and then. Boil about as many nice young peas as would make a dish, the same as for eating; put them in about ten minutes before you take it up, skimming all the fat nicely off; and season it at the same time with salt and cayenne to your taste.

Another way.

Cut your veal into pieces, about three inches long; fry it delicately; mix a little flour with some beef broth, with an onion and two cloves; stew this some time, strain it, add three pints or two quarts of peas, or heads of asparagus, cut like peas. Put in the meat; let it stew gently; add pepper and salt.

Breast of Veal ragout.

Bone and cut out a large square piece of the breast of veal; cut the rest into small pieces, and brown it in butter, stewing it in your ragout for made dishes; thicken it with brown butter, and put the ragout in the dish. Lay diced lemon, sweetbreads, sippets, and bacon, fried in batter of eggs; then lay on the square piece. Garnish with sliced oranges.

Veal Collops, with Oysters.

Cut thin slices out of a leg of veal, as many as will make a dish, according to the number of your company. Lard one quarter of them, and fry them in butter; take them out of the pan and keep them warm. Clean the pan, and put into it half a pint of oysters, with their liquor, and some strong broth, one or two shalots, a glass of white wine, two or three anchovies minced, and some grated nutmeg; let these have a boil up, and thicken with five eggs and a piece of butter. Put in your collops, and shake them together till the sauce is tolerably thick. Set them on the stove again to stew a little; then serve up.

Veal Collops, with white sauce.

Cut veal that has been already roasted into neat small pieces, round or square; season them with a little pepper and salt; pass them quick of a pale colour in a bit of butter of the size of a walnut; add the yolks of five eggs, and half a pint of cream, with a very small onion or two, previously boiled; toss them up quick, and serve hot.

Veal Cutlets, to dress.

Cut the veal steaks thin; hack and season them with pepper, salt, and sweet-herbs. Wash them over with melted butter, and wrap white paper buttered over them. Roast or bake them; and, when done, take off the paper, and serve them with good gravy and Seville orange-juice squeezed on.

Another way.

Take the best end of a neck of veal and cut your cutlets; four ribs will make eight cutlets. Beat them out very thin, and trim them round. Take chopped parsley, thyme, shalots, and mushrooms, pass them over the fire, add a little juice of lemon, lemon-peel, and grated nutmeg. Dip in the cutlets, crumb them, and boil them over a gentle fire. Save what you leave from dipping them in, put some brown sauce to it, and put it under them when going to table, first taking care to remove the grease from it. Lamb cutlets are done the same way.

Veal Cutlets, larded.

Cut a neck of veal into bones; lard one side, and fry them off quick. Thicken a piece of butter, of the size of a large nut, with a little flour, and whole onion. Put in as much good gravy as will just cover them, and a few mushrooms and forcemeat balls. Stove them tender; skim off all grease; squeeze in half a lemon, and serve them up.

Fillet of Veal, to farce or roast.

Mince some beef suet very small, with some sweet marjoram, winter savory, and thyme; season with salt, cloves, and mace, well beaten; put in grated bread; mix them all together with the yolk of an egg; make small holes in the veal, and stuff it very thick with these. Put it on the spit and roast it well. Let the sauce consist of butter, gravy, and juice of lemon, very thick. Dish the veal, and pour the sauce over it, with slices of lemon laid round the dish.

Fillet of Veal, to boil.

Cut out the bone of a fillet of veal; put it into good milk and water for a little while: make some forcemeat with boiled clary, raw carrots, beef suet, grated bread, sweet-herbs, and a good quantity of shrimps, nutmeg, and mace, the yolks of three eggs boiled hard, some pepper and salt, and two raw eggs; roll it up in butter, and stuff the veal with it. Boil the veal in a cloth for two hours, and scald four or five cucumbers, in order to take out the pulp the more easily. This done, fill them with forcemeat, and stew them in a little thin gravy. For sauce take strong white gravy, thickened with butter, a very little flour, nutmeg, mace, and lemon-peel, three anchovies dissolved in lemon-juice, some good cream, the yolk of an egg beaten, and a glass of white wine. Serve with the cucumbers.

Half a Fillet of Veal, to stew.

Take a stewpan large enough for the piece of veal, put in some butter, and fry it till it is firm, and of a fine brown colour all round; put in two carrots, two large onions, whole, half a pound of lean bacon, a bunch of thyme and of parsley, a pinch of cayenne pepper and of salt: add a cupful of broth, and let the whole stew over a very slow fire for one hour, or according to the size of your piece of veal, until thoroughly done. Have ready a pint of jelly soup, in which stew a table-spoonful of mustard and the same of truffles cut in small pieces; add one ounce of butter and a dessert spoonful of flour to thicken; unite it well together; put in a glass of white wine, and boil. When ready to serve, pour it over the veal; let there be sauce sufficient to fill the dish; the veal must be strained from the vegetables, and great care taken that the sauce is well passed through the sieve, to keep it clear from grease.

Knuckle of Veal, white.

Boil a knuckle of veal in a little water kept close from the air, with six onions and a little whole pepper, till tender. The sauce to be poured over it, when dished in a little of its own liquor—two or three anchovies, a little mace, half a pint of cream, and the yolk of an egg, thickened with a little flour.

Knuckle of Veal ragout.

Cut the veal into slices half an inch thick; pepper, salt, and flour them; fry them of a light brown; put the trimmings, with the bone broken, an onion sliced, celery, a bunch of sweet-herbs; pour warm water to cover them about an inch. Stew gently for two hours; strain it, and thicken with flour and butter, a spoonful of ketchup, a glass of wine, and the juice of half a lemon. Give it a boil, strain into a clean saucepan, put in the meat, and make it hot.

Leg of Veal and Bacon, to boil.

Lard the veal with bacon and lemon-peel; boil it with a piece of bacon, cut in slices; put the veal into a dish, and lay the bacon round it. Serve it up with green sauce made thus: beat two or more handfuls of sorrel in a mortar, with two pippins quartered, and put vinegar and sugar to it.

Loin of Veal, to roast.

Roast, and baste with butter; set a dish under your veal, with vinegar, a few sage leaves, and a little rosemary and thyme. Let the gravy drop on these, and, when the veal is roasted, let the herbs and gravy boil once or twice on the fire: serve it under the veal.

Loin of Veal, to roast with herbs.

Lard the fillet of a loin of veal; put it into an earthen pan; steep it three hours with parsley, scallions, a little fennel, mushrooms, a laurel-leaf, thyme, basil, and two shalots, the whole shred very fine, salt, whole pepper, a little grated nutmeg, and a little sweet oil. When it has taken the flavour of the herbs, put it upon the spit, with all its seasoning, wrapt in two sheets of white paper well buttered; tie it carefully so as to prevent the herbs falling out, and roast it at a very slow fire. When it is done take off the paper, and with a knife pick off all the bits of herbs that stick to the meat and paper, and put them into a stewpan, with a little gravy, two spoonfuls of verjuice, salt, whole pepper, and a bit of butter, about as big as a walnut, rolled in flour. Before you thicken the sauce, melt a little butter; mix it with the yolk of an egg, and rub the outside of the veal, which should then be covered with grated bread, and browned with a salamander. Serve it up with a good sauce under, but not poured over so as to disturb the meat.

Loin of Veal, fricassee of.

Well roast a loin of veal, and let it stand till cold. Cut it into slices; in a saucepan over the stove melt some butter, with a little flour, shred parsley, and chives. Turn the stewpan a little for a minute or so, and pepper and salt the veal. Put it again into the pan, and give it three or four turns over the stove with a little broth, and boil it a little: then put three or four yolks of eggs beaten up to a cream, and some parsley shred, to thicken it, always keeping it stirred over the fire till of sufficient thickness; then serve it up.

Loin of Veal Bechamel.

When the veal is nicely roasted, cut out part of the fillet down the back; cut it in thin slices, and put some white sauce to what you have cut out. Season it with the juice of lemon and a little pepper and salt; put it into the veal, and cover the top with crumbs of bread that has been browned, or salamander it over with crumbs, or leave the skin of the veal so that you can turn it over when the seasoning part is put in.

Neck of Veal, stewed with Celery.

Take the best end of a neck, put it into a stewpan with beef broth, salt, whole pepper, and two cloves, tied in a bit of muslin, an onion, and a piece of lemon-peel. Add a little cream and flour mixed, some celery ready boiled, and cut into lengths; and boil it up.

Veal Olives. No. 1.

are done the same way as the beef olives, only cut off a fillet of veal, fried of a fine brown. The same sauce is used as for beef, and, if you like, small bits of curled bacon may be laid in the dish. Garnish with lemon and parsley.

Veal Olives. No. 2.

Wash eight or ten Scots collops over with egg batter; season and lay over a little forcemeat; roll them up and roast them; make a good ragout for them; garnish with sliced orange.

Veal Olives. No. 3.

Take a good fillet of veal, and cut large collops, not too thin, and hack them well; wash them over with the yolk of an egg; then spread on a good layer of forcemeat, made of veal pretty well seasoned. Roll them up, and wash them with egg; lard them over with fat bacon, tie them round, if you roast them; but, if to be baked, you need only wash the bacon over with egg. Garnish with slices of lemon, and for sauce take thick butter and good gravy, with a piece of lemon.

Veal Olives. No. 4.

Lay over your forcemeat; first lard your collops, and lay a row of large oysters; and then roll them up, and roast or bake them. Make a ragout of oysters, sweetbreads fried, a few morels and mushrooms, and lay in the bottom of your dish, and garnish with fried oysters and grated bread.

Veal Rumps.

Take three veal rumps; parboil and put them into a little pot, with some broth, a bunch of parsley, scallions, a clove of garlic, two shalots, a laurel leaf, thyme, basil, two cloves, salt, pepper, an onion, a carrot, and a parsnip: let them boil till they are thoroughly done, and the sauce is very nearly consumed. Take them out, let them cool, and strain the sauce through a rather coarse sieve, that none of the fat may remain. Put it into a stewpan, with the yolks of three eggs beat up, and a little flour, and thicken it over the fire. Then dip your veal rumps into it, and cover them with grated bread; put them upon a dish, and brown them with a salamander. Serve them with sour sauce, for which see the part that treats of [Sauces]().

Shoulder of Veal, to stew.

Put it in an earthen pan, with a gill of water, two spoonfuls of vinegar, salt, whole pepper, parsley and scallions, two cloves of garlic, a bay leaf, two onions, two heads of celery, three cloves, and a bit of butter. Cover the pan close, and close the edges with flour and water. Stew it in an oven three hours; then skim and strain the sauce, and serve it over the veal.

Veal Steaks.

Cut a neck of veal into steaks, and beat them on both sides: beat up an egg, and with a feather wet your steaks on both sides. Add some parsley, thyme, and a little marjoram, cut small, and seasoned with pepper and salt. Sprinkle crumbs of bread on both sides of the steaks, and put them up quite tight and close into paper which has been rubbed with butter. They may be either broiled or baked in a pan.

Veal Sweetbreads, to fry.

Cut each of your sweetbreads in three or four pieces and blanch them: put them for two hours in a marinade made with lemon-juice, salt, pepper, cloves, a bay leaf, and an onion sliced. Take the sweetbreads out of the marinade, and dry them with a cloth; dip them in beaten yolk of eggs, with crumbs of bread; fry them in lard till they are brown; drain them; fry some parsley, and put it in the middle of the dish, and serve them.

Veal Sweetbreads, to roast.

Lard your sweetbreads with small lardoons of bacon, and put them on a skewer; fasten them to the spit and roast them brown. Put some good gravy into a dish; lay in the sweetbreads, and serve them very hot. You ought to set your sweetbreads and spit them; then egg and bread them, or they will not be brown.

Vegetables, to stew.

Cut some onions, celery, turnips, and carrots, into small squares, like dice, but not too small; stew them with a bunch of thyme in a little broth and butter; fry them till they are of a fine brown colour; turn them with a fork, till quite soft; if they are not done enough, put a little flour from the dredging-box to brown them; skim the sauce well, and pass it through a sieve; add a little cayenne pepper and salt; put the vegetables in, and serve them up.

Haunch of Venison, to roast. No. 1.

Butter and sprinkle your fat with salt; lay a sheet of paper over it; roll a thin sheet of paste and again another sheet of paper over the paste, and with a packthread tie and spit it. Baste the sheet of paper with butter, and let the venison roast till done enough. Be careful how you take off the papers and paste, basting it with some butter during that time, and dredge up: then let it turn round some time to give the fat a colour. The object of pasting is to save the fat. Have currant-jelly with it, and serve it up.

Haunch of Venison, to roast. No. 2.

Let your haunch be well larded with thick bacon; seasoning it with fine spices, parsley, sweet-herbs, cut small, pepper, and salt. Pickle it with vinegar, onions, salt, pepper, parsley, sweet basil, thyme, and bay-leaves: and, when pickled enough, spit it, and baste it with the pickle. When roasted, dish it up with vinegar, pepper, and thick sauce.

Haunch of Venison, to roast. No. 3.

Have the haunch well and finely larded with bacon, and put paper round it: roast and serve it up with sauce under it, made of good cullis or broth, gravy of ham, capers, anchovies, salt, pepper, and vinegar.

Venison, to boil.

Have your venison a little salted, and boil it in water. Meanwhile boil six cauliflowers in milk and water; and put them into a large pipkin with drawn butter; keep them warm, and put in six handfuls of washed spinach, boiled in strong broth; pour off the broth, and put some drawn butter to it; lay some sippets in the dish, and lay your spinach round the sides; have the venison laid in the middle, with the cauliflower over it; pour your butter also over, and garnish with barberries and minced parsley.

Haunch of Venison, to broil.

Take half a haunch, and cut it into slices of about half an inch thick; broil and salt them over a brisk fire, and, when pretty well soaked, bread and serve them up with gravy: do the same with the chine.

Venison, to recover when tainted.

Boil bay salt, ale, and vinegar together, and make a strong brine; skim it, and let it stand till cool, and steep the venison for a whole day. Drain and press it dry: parboil, and season it with pepper and salt.

Another way.

Tie your venison up in a clean cloth; put it in the earth for a whole day, and the scent will be gone.

Red Deer Venison, to pot.

Let the venison be well boned and cut into pieces about an inch thick, and round, of the diameter of your pot. Season with pepper and salt, something higher than you would pasty, and afterwards put it into your pots, adding half a quarter of butter, and two sliced nutmegs, cloves and mace about the same quantity of each, but rather less of the cloves. Then put into your pots lean and fat, so that there may be fat and lean mixed, until the pots are so nearly filled as to admit only a pint of butter more to be put into each. Make a paste of rye-flour, and stop your pots close on the top. Have your oven heated as you would for a pasty; put your pots in, and let them remain as long as for pasty; draw them out, and let them stand half an hour; afterwards unstop them, and turn the pots upside down; you may remove the contents, if you like, into smaller pots; in which case take off all the butter, letting the gravy remain, and using the butter for the fresh pots; let them remain all night; the next day fill them with fresh butter. To make a pie of the same, proceed in the same way with the venison, only do not season it so high; but put in a liberal allowance of butter.

Venison, excellent substitute for.

POULTRY.

Chicken, to make white.

Feed them in the coop on boiled rice; give them no water at all to drink. Scalded oatmeal will do as well.

Chicken, to fricassee. No. 1.

Empty the chicken, and singe it till the flesh gets very firm. Carve it as neatly as possible; divide the legs at the joints into four separate pieces, the back into two, making in all ten pieces. Take out the lungs and all that remains within; wash all the parts of the chicken very thoroughly in lukewarm water, till all the blood is out. Put the pieces in boiling water, sufficient to cover them, about four tea-cupfuls, and let them remain there ten minutes; take them out, preserve the water, and put them into cold water. When quite cool, put two ounces of fresh butter into a stewpan with half a pint of mushrooms, fresh or pickled; if pickled, they must be put into fresh cold water two or three hours before; the water to be changed three times; put into the stewpan two bunches of parsley and two large onions; add the chicken, and set the stewpan over the fire. When the chickens have been fried lightly, taking care they are not in the least browned, dust a little salt and flour over them; then add some veal jelly to the water in which they were blanched; let them boil about three quarters of an hour in that liquor, skimming off all the butter, and scum very cleanly; then take out the chicken, leaving the sauce or liquor, and lay it in another stewpan, which place in a basin of hot water near the fire. Boil down the sauce or liquor, adding some more veal jelly, till it becomes strong, and there remains sufficient sauce for the dish; add to this the yolk of four eggs and three table-spoonfuls of cream: boil it, taking great care to keep it constantly stirring; and, when ready to serve, having placed the chicken in a very hot dish, with the breast in the middle, and the legs around, pour the sauce well over every part. The sauce should be thicker than melted butter, and of a yellow colour.

Chicken, to fricassee. No. 2.

Cut the chicken up in joints; put them into cold water, and set them on the fire till they boil; skim them well. Save the liquor. Skin, wash, and trim the joints; put them into a pan, with the liquor, a small bunch of parsley and thyme, a small onion, and as much flour and water as will give it a proper thickness, and let them boil till tender. When going to table, put in a yolk of egg mixed with a little good cream, a little parsley chopped very fine, juice of lemon, and pepper and salt to your taste.

Chicken, to fricassee. No. 3.

Take two chickens and more than half stew them; cut them into limbs; take the skin clean off, and all the inside that is bloody. Put them into a stewpan, with half a pint of cream, about two ounces of butter, into which shake a little flour, some mace, and whole pepper, and a little parsley boiled and chopped fine. Thicken it up with the yolks of two eggs; add the juice of a lemon, and three spoonfuls of good white gravy.

Chicken, to fricassee. No. 4.

Have a frying-pan, with sufficient liquor to cover your chicken cut into pieces; half of the liquor to be white wine and water. Take one nutmeg sliced, half a dozen cloves, three blades of mace, and some whole pepper; boil all these together in a frying-pan; put half a pound of fresh butter and skim it clean; then put in your chickens, and boil them till tender; add a small quantity of parsley. Take four yolks and two whites of eggs; beat them well with some thick butter, and put it to your chicken in the pan; toss it over a slow fire till thick, and serve it up with sippets.

Chicken, white fricassee of.

Cut in pieces chickens or rabbits; wash and dry them in a cloth; flour them well, and fry in clarified butter till they are a little brown, but, if not enough done, put them in a stewpan, and just cover them with strong veal or beef broth. Put in with them a bunch of thyme, an onion stuck with cloves, a little pepper and salt, and a blade of mace. Cover and stew till tender, and till the liquor is reduced about one half. Put in a quarter of a pound of butter, the yolk of two eggs beat, and a quarter of a pint of cream. Stir well; let it boil; if not thick enough, shake in some flour; and then put in juice of lemon.

Cream of Chicken, or Fowl.

For this purpose fowls are preferable, because the breasts are larger. Take two chickens, cut off the breast, and roast them; the remainder put in a stewpan with two pounds of the sinewy part of a knuckle of veal. Boil the whole together to make a little clear good broth: when the breasts are roasted, and your broth made, take all the white of the breast, put it in a small stewpan, and add to it the broth clean and clear. It will be better to cut the white of the chickens quite fine, and, when you find that it is boiled soft, proceed in the same manner as for cream of rice and pass it. Just in the same way, make it of the thickness you judge proper, and warm in the same manner as the cream of rice: put in a little salt if it is approved of.

Chickens, to fry.

Scald and split them; put them in vinegar and water, as much as will cover them, with a little pepper and salt, an onion, a slice or two of lemon, and a sprig or two of thyme, and let them lie two hours in the pickle. Dry them with a cloth; flour and fry them in clarified butter, with soft bread and a little of the pickle.

Chickens, to heat.

Take the legs, wings, brains, and rump, and put them into a little white wine vinegar and claret, with some fresh butter, the water of an onion, a little pepper and sliced nutmeg, and heat them between two dishes.

Chickens, dressed with Peas.

Singe and truss your chickens; boil one half and roast the other. Put them into a small saucepan, with a little water, a small piece of butter, a little salt, and a bundle of thyme and parsley. Set them on the fire, and put in a small lump of sugar. When they boil, set them over a slow fire to stew. Lay your boiled chickens in a dish; put your peas over them; then lay the roasted ones between, and send to table.

Chicken and Ham, ragout of.

Clear a chicken which has been dressed of all the sauce that may be about it. If it has been roasted, pare off the brown skin, take some soup, veal jelly, and cream, and a table-spoonful of mushrooms; if pickled, wash them in several waters to take out the vinegar: put them in the jelly, and keep this sauce to heat up. Cut up the chicken, the wings and breast in slices, the merrythought also, and divide the legs. Heat the fowl up separately from the sauce in a little thin broth: prepare six or eight slices of ham stewed apart in brown gravy; dip each piece of the fowl in the white sauce, and lay them in the middle of the dish with a piece of the ham alternately one beside another, taking care that as little of the white sauce as possible goes on the ham, to preserve its colour. Lay the legs one on each side of the meat in the middle; and pour the sauce in the middle, taking care not to pour it over the ham.

Chicken, or Ham and Veal patés.

Cut up into small dice some of the white of the chicken, or the most delicate part of veal already dressed; take sufficient white sauce, with truffles, morels, and mushrooms, and heat it up to put in the patés. When ready, pour it amply into them, and serve up hot.

Another.

Take the white of a chicken or veal, cut it up in small dice; do the same with some ham or tongue; warm it in a little broth, and take a good white sauce, such as is used for pheasants, and heat it up thoroughly.

Duck, to boil.

Pour over it boiling milk and water, and let it lie for an hour or two. Then boil it gently for a full half hour in plenty of water. Serve with onion sauce.

Duck, to boil, à la Française.

To a pint of rich beef gravy put two dozen of roasted peeled chesnuts, with a few leaves of thyme, two small onions if agreeable, a race of ginger, and a little whole pepper. Lard a fine tame duck, and half roast it; put it into the gravy; let it stew ten minutes, and add a pint of port wine. When the duck is done, take it out; boil up your gravy to a proper thickness, but skim it very clean from the fat; lay your duck in the dish, and pour the sauce over it.

Duck à la braise.

Lard the duck; lay a slice or two of beef at the bottom of the pan, and on these the duck, a piece of bacon, and some more beef sliced, an onion, a carrot, whole pepper, a slice of lemon, and a bunch of sweet-herbs. Cover this close, and set it over the fire for a few minutes, shaking in some flour: then pour in a quart of beef broth or boiling water, and a little heated red wine. Stew it for half an hour; strain the sauce, and skim it; put to it some more wine if necessary, with cayenne, shalot, a little mint, juice of a lemon, and chopped tarragon. If agreeable to your taste, add artichoke bottoms boiled and quartered.

Duck, to hash.

When cut in pieces, flour it; put it into a stewpan with some gravy, a little red wine, shalot chopped, salt and pepper; boil these; put in the duck; toss it up, take out the lemon, and serve with toasted sippets.

Duck, to stew with Cucumbers.

Half roast the duck, and stew it as before. Slice some cucumbers and onions; fry and drain them very dry; put them to the duck, and stew all together.

Duck, to stew with Peas.

Half roast the duck, put it into some good gravy with a little mint and three or four sage-leaves chopped. Stew this half an hour; thicken the gravy with a little flour; throw in half a pint of green peas boiled, or some celery, in which case omit the mint.

Fowls, to fatten in a fortnight.

Gather and dry, in proper season, nettle leaves and seed; beat them into powder, and make it into paste with flour, adding a little sweet olive-oil. Make this up into small crams: coop the birds up and feed them with it, giving them water in which barley has been boiled, and they will fatten in the above-mentioned time.

Fowl, to make tender.

Pour down the throat of the fowl, about an hour before you kill it, a spoonful of vinegar, and let it run about again. When killed, hang it up in the feathers by the legs in a smoky chimney; then pluck and dress it. This method makes fowls very tender.

Fowl, to roast with Anchovies.

Put a bit of butter in your stewpan with a little flour; keep stirring this over the fire, but not too hot, till it turns of a good gold colour, and put a little of it into your gravy to thicken it.

Fowl with Rice, called Pilaw.

Boil a pint of rice in as much water as will cover it. Put in with it some whole black pepper, a little salt, and half a dozen cloves, tied up in a bit of cloth. When the rice is tender take out the cloves and pepper, and stir in a piece of butter. Boil a fowl and a piece of bacon; lay them in a dish, and cover them with the rice. Lay round the dish and upon the rice hard eggs cut in halves and quarters, and onions, first boiled and then fried.

Fowl, to hash.

Cut the fowl in pieces; put it in some gravy, with a little cream, ketchup, or mushroom-powder, grated lemon-peel, a few oysters and their liquor, and a piece of butter mixed with flour. Keep stirring it till the butter is melted. Lay sippets in the dish.

Fowl, to stew.

Take a fowl, two onions, two carrots, and two turnips; put one onion into the fowl, and cut all the rest into four pieces each. Add two or three bits of bacon or ham, a bay-leaf, and as much water as will prevent their burning when put into an earthen vessel; cover them up close, and stew them for three hours and a half on a slow fire. Serve up hot or cold.

Goose, to stuff.

Having well washed your goose, dry it, and rub the inside with pepper and salt. Crumble some bread, but not too fine; take a piece of butter and make it hot; cut a middle-sized onion and stew in the butter. Cut the liver very small, and put that also in the butter for about a minute just to warm, and pour it over the head. It must then be mixed up with an egg and about two spoonfuls of cream, a little nutmeg, ginger, pepper and salt, and a small quantity of summer savory.

Another way.

Chop fine two ounces of onions, and an ounce of green sage leaves; add four ounces of bread crumbs, the yolk and white of an egg, a little salt and pepper, and sometimes minced apples.

Goose's liver, to dress.

When it is drawn, leave the gall sticking to it; lay it in fresh water for a day, and change the water several times. When you use it, wipe it dry, cut off the gall, and fry it in butter, which must be made very hot before the liver is put in: it must be whole and fried brown—no fork stuck in it. Serve with a little ketchup sauce.

Pigeons, to boil.

Chop sweet-herbs and bacon, with grated bread, butter, spice, and the yolk of an egg; tie both ends of the pullets, and boil them. Garnish with sliced lemon and barberries.

Pigeons, to broil.

Cut their necks and wings close, leaving the skin of the neck to enable you to tie close, and with some grated bread put an anchovy, the two livers of pigeons, half a grated nutmeg, a quarter of a pound of butter, a very little thyme, a little pepper and salt, and sweet marjoram shred. Mix all together, and into each bird put a piece of the size of a walnut, after sewing up the vents and necks, and, with a little nutmeg, pepper, and salt, strewed over them, broil them on a slow charcoal fire, basting and turning very often. Use rich gravy or melted butter for sauce, and season to your taste.

Pigeons, to jug.

Pick and draw the pigeons, and let a little water pass through them; parboil and bruise the liver with a spoon; mix pepper, salt, grated nutmeg, parsley shred fine, and lemon-peel, suet cut small, in quantity equal to the liver, the yolks of two eggs boiled hard and also cut fine; mix these with two raw eggs, and stuff the birds, tying up the necks and vents. After dipping the pigeons into water, season them with salt and pepper; then put them into a jug, with two or three pieces of celery, stopping it very close, to prevent the steam escaping. Set them in a kettle of cold water; lay a tile on the top, and boil three hours; take them out, and put in a piece of butter rolled in flour; shake it round till thick, and pour it over the pigeons.

Pigeons, to pot.

Truss and season them with savoury spice; put them into a a pot or pan, covering them with butter, and bake them. Take out, drain, and, when cold, cover them with clarified butter. Fish may be potted in the same way, but always bone them when baked.

Pigeons, to stew. No. 1.

Truss your pigeons as for boiling. Take pepper, salt, cloves, mace, some sweet-herbs, a little grated bread, and the liver of the birds chopped very fine; roll these up in a bit of butter, put it in the stomach of the pigeons, and tie up both ends. Make some butter hot in your stewpan, fry the pigeons in it till they are brown all over, putting to them two or three blades of mace, a few peppercorns, and one shalot. Take them out of the liquor, dust a little flour into the stewpan, shaking it about till it is brown. Have ready a quart of small gravy and a glass of white wine; let it just boil up: strain out all the spice, and put the gravy and pigeons into the stewpan. Let them simmer over the fire two hours; put in some pickled mushrooms, a little lemon juice, a spoonful of ketchup, a few truffles and morels. Dish and send to table with bits of bacon grilled. Some persons add forcemeat balls, but they are very rich without.

Pigeons, to stew. No. 2.

Shred the livers and gizzards, with as much suet as there is meat; season with pepper, salt, parsley, and thyme, shred small; fill the pigeons with this stuffing; lay them in the stewpan, breasts downward, with as much strong broth as will cover them. Add pepper, salt, and onion, and two thin rashers of bacon. Cover them close; let them stew two hours or more, till the liquor is reduced to one half, and looks like gravy, and the pigeons are tender; then put them in a dish with sippets. If you have no strong broth, you may stew in water; but you must not put so much water as broth, and they must stew more slowly.

Pigeons, to stew. No. 3.

Cut six pigeons with giblets into quarters, and put them into a stewpan, with two blades of mace, salt, pepper, and just water sufficient to stew them without burning. When tender, thicken the liquor with the yolk of an egg and three spoonfuls of fresh cream, a little shred thyme, parsley, and a bit of butter. Shake all together, and garnish with lemon.

Pigeons, biscuit of.

Wash, clean, and parboil, your pigeons, and stew them in strong broth. Have a ragout made for them of strong gravy, with artichoke bottoms and onions, seasoning them with the juice of lemons, and lemons diced, truffles, mushrooms, morels, and bacon cut as for lard. Pour the broth into a dish with dried sippets, and, after placing your pigeons, pour on the ragout. Garnish with scalded parsley, lemons, and beet-root.

Pigeons, en compote. No. 1.

The pigeons must be young and white, and the inside entirely taken out. Let none of the heart or liver remain, which is apt to render them bitter. Make some forcemeat of veal, and fill the pigeons with it; then put them in a braise, with some bacon, a slice of lemon, a little thyme, and bay-leaf, and let them stew gently for an hour. The sauce is made of cucumbers and mushrooms, and they must be sweated in a little butter till tender; then strain it off the butter, and put in some strong gravy and a little flour to thicken it. Lastly, add the yolks of two eggs and a little good cream, which, when put to it, must be well stirred, and not suffered to boil, as it would curdle and spoil the sauce.

Pigeons, en compote. No. 2.

Have the birds trussed with their legs in their bodies, but stuffed with forcemeat; parboil and lard them with fat bacon; season with pepper, spices, parsley, and minced chives; stew them very gently. While they are stewing, make a ragout of fowls' livers, cocks'-combs, truffles, morels, and mushrooms, and put a little bacon in the frying-pan to melt; put them in, and shake the pan three or four times round; then add some rich gravy, and let it simmer a little, and put in some veal cullis and ham to thicken it. Drain the pigeons, and put them into this ragout; let them just simmer; take them up, put them into your dish, and pour the ragout over.

Pigeons, en compote. No. 3.

Lard, truss, and force them; season and stew them in strong broth. Have a ragout garnished with sippets, sweetbreads, and sprigs of parsley; then fry the pigeons in a batter of eggs and sliced bacon. You may garnish most dishes in the same way.

Pigeons, à la Crapaudine.

Cut the birds open down the back, and draw the legs through the skin inside, as you would do a boiled fowl, then put into a roomy saucepan some butter, a little parsley, thyme, shalots, and, if you can have them, mushrooms, all chopped together very fine. Put the pigeons in this, and let them sweat in the butter and herbs for about five minutes. While they are warm and moist with the herbs and butter, cover them all over with fine bread crumbs; sprinkle a little salt upon them, and boil them on a slow fire. The sauce may be either of mushrooms or cucumbers, made by sweating whichever you choose in butter till quite tender, then adding a little gravy, cream, and flour.

Pigeons in disguise.

Draw, truss, and season the pigeons with salt and pepper, and make a nice puff; roll each pigeon in a piece of it; tie them in a cloth, but be careful not to let the paste break. Boil them in plenty of water for an hour and a half; and when you untie them take great care they do not break; put them into a dish, and pour a little good gravy to them.

Pigeons in fricandeau.

Draw and truss the pigeons with the legs in the bellies, larding them with bacon, and slit them. Fry them of a fine brown in butter: put into the stewpan a quart of good gravy, a little lemon-pickle, a tea-spoonful of walnut ketchup, cayenne, a little salt, a few truffles, morels, and some yolks of hard eggs. Pour your sauce with its ingredients over the pigeons, when laid in the dish.

Pigeons aux Poires.

Let the feet be cut off, and stuff them with forcemeat, in the shape of a pear, rolling them in the yolk of an egg and crumbs of bread, putting in at the lower end to make them look like pears. Rub your dish with a piece of butter, and then lay them over it, but not to touch each other, and bake them. When done, lay them in another dish, and pour some good gravy into it, thickening with the yolk of an egg; but take care not to pour it over the pigeons.

Another way.

Cut off one leg; truss the pigeons to boil, and let the leg come out of the vent; fill them with forcemeat: tie them with packthread, and stew them in good broth. Roll the pigeons in yolks of eggs, well beaten with crumbs of bread. Lard your stewpan, but not too hot, and fry your birds to the colour of a popling pear; lay them in a dish, and send up gravy and orange in a terrine with them.

Pigeons, Pompeton of.

Butter your pan, lay in it some sliced bacon, and cover all the inside of it with forcemeat. Brown the pigeons off in a pan, and put them in a good ragout, stewing them up together, and put also a good ladleful of ragout to the forcemeat: then lay your pigeons breast downward, and pour over them the ragout that remains; cover them with forcemeat, and bake them. Turn them out, and serve up.

Pigeons au Soleil.

Make some forcemeat, with half a pound of veal, a quarter of a pound of mutton, and two ounces of beef, and beat them in a mortar with salt, pepper, and mace, till they become paste. Beat up the yolks of four eggs, put them into a plate, and mix two ounces of flour and a quarter of a pound of grated bread. Set on your stewpan with a little rich beef gravy; tie up three or four cloves in a piece of muslin, and put into it; then put your pigeons in, and stew them till nearly done; set them before the fire to keep warm, and with some good beef dripping in your pan, enough to cover the birds, set it on the fire; when boiling, take one at a time, and roll it in the meat that was beaten, then in the yolk of an egg, till they are quite wet; strew them with bread and flour in boiling dripping, and let them remain till brown.

Pigeons à la Tatare, with Cold Sauce.

Singe and truss the pigeons as for boiling, and beat them flat, but not so as to break the skin; season them with salt, pepper, cloves, and mace. Dip them in melted butter and grated bread; lay them on a gridiron, and turn them often. Should the fire not be clear, lay them upon a sheet of paper buttered, to keep them from being smoked. For sauce, take a piece of onion or shalot, an anchovy, and two spoonfuls of pickled cucumbers, capers, and mushrooms: mince these very small by themselves; add a little pepper and salt, five spoonfuls of oil, one of water, and the juice of a lemon, and mix them well together with mustard. Pour the sauce cold into the dish, and lay the birds, when broiled, upon it.

Pigeons, Surtout of.

Take some large tame pigeons; make forcemeat thus: parboil and bruise the livers fine; beat some boiled ham in a mortar; mix these with some mushrooms, a little chopped parsley, a clove of garlic shred fine, two or three young onions minced fine, a sweetbread of veal, parboiled and minced very fine, pepper, and salt. Fill the pigeons with this stuffing; tie them close, and cover each pigeon with the forcemeat: tie them up in paper to keep it on, and while roasting have some essence of ham heated; pour it into your dish, and lay your pigeons upon it.

To preserve tainted Poultry.

Have a large cask that has been just emptied, with part of a stave or two knocked out at the head, and into the others drive hooks to hang your fowls, but not so as to touch one another, covering the open places with the staves or boards already knocked out, but leaving the bung-hole open as an air vent. Let them dry in a cool place, and in this way you may keep fish or flesh.

Pullets with Oysters.

Boil your pullets. Put a quart of oysters over the fire till they are set; strain them through a sieve, saving the liquor, and put into it two or three blades of mace, with a little thyme, an onion, parsley, and two anchovies. Boil and strain all these off, together with half a pound of butter; draw it up, and squeeze into it half a lemon. Then let the oysters be washed, and set one by one in cold water; put them in the liquor, having made it very hot, and pour it over the pullets. Garnish, if you please, with bacon and sausages.

Pullets to bone and farce.

Bone the pullets as whole as you possibly can, and fill the belly with sweetbreads, mushrooms, chesnuts, and forcemeat balls; lard the breast with gross lard, pass them off in a pan, and either roast or stew them, making a sauce with mushrooms and oysters, and lay them under.

Rabbits, to boil.

Truss and lard them with bacon, boiling them white. Take the liver, shred with it fat bacon for sauce, and put to it very strong broth, vinegar, white wine, salt, nutmeg, mace, minced parsley, barberries, and drawn butter. Lay your rabbits in the dish, and let the sauce be poured over them. Garnish the dish with barberries and lemon.

Rabbits, to boil with Onions.

Truss the rabbits close; well wash; boil them white; boil the onions by themselves, changing the water three times. Strain them well, and chop and butter them, putting in a quarter of a pint of cream; then serve up the rabbits covered with onions.

Rabbits, brown fricassee of.

Fry your rabbits brown, and stew it in some gravy, with thyme, an onion, and parsley, tied together. Season, and thicken it with brown thickening, a few morels, mushrooms, lemon, and forcemeat balls.

Rabbits, white fricassee of. No. 1.

Cut the rabbits in slices; wash away the blood; fry them on a slow fire, and put them into your pan with a little strong broth; seasoning, and tossing them up with oysters and mushrooms. When almost done, put in a pint of cream, thickened with a piece of butter and flour.

Rabbits, white fricassee of. No. 2.

Take the yolks of five eggs and a pint of cream; beat them together, and put two ounces of butter into the cream, until the rabbits are tender. Put in this liquor to the rabbits, and keep tossing them over the fire till they become thickened, and then squeeze in a lemon; add truffles, mushrooms, morels, artichoke bottoms, pallets, cocks-combs, forcemeat balls, or any of these.

Rabbits, white fricassee of. No. 3.

Cut them in the same manner as for eating, and put them into a stewpan, with a pint of veal gravy, a little beaten mace, a slice of lemon-peel, and anchovy, and season with cayenne pepper and salt. Stew over a slow fire, and, when done enough, thicken the gravy with butter and flour; then strain and add to it two eggs, mixed with a glass of cream, and a little nutmeg. Take care not to let it boil.

Turkey, to boil.

Fill a large turkey with oysters; take a breast of veal, cut in olives; bone it, and season it with pepper, salt, nutmegs, cloves, mace, lemon-peel, and thyme, cut small; take some lean veal to make forcemeat, with the ingredients before mentioned, only adding shalot and anchovies; put some in the olives and some in the turkey, in a cloth; roast or bake the olives. Take three anchovies, a little pepper, a quarter of a pint of gravy, as much white wine; boil these with a little thyme till half is consumed; then put in some butter, meat, oysters, mushrooms, fried balls, and bacon; put all these in a pan, and pour on the turkey; lay the olives round, and garnish the dish with pickles and lemon. If you want sauce, add a little gravy, and serve it up.

Turkey, with Oysters.

Boil your turkey, and serve with the same sauce as for pullets, only adding a few mushrooms.

Turkey à la Daube.

Bone a turkey, and season it with pepper and salt; spread over it some slices of ham, over them some forcemeat, over that a fowl, boned, and seasoned as the turkey, then more ham and forcemeat, and sew it up. Cover the bottom of a stewpan with veal and ham cut in slices; lay in the turkey breast downward: chop all the bones to pieces, and lay them on the turkey; cover the pan close, and set it over the fire for five minutes. Put as much clear broth as will cover it, and let it do for two hours. When it is more than half done, put in one ounce of the best isinglass and a bundle of sweet-herbs; skim off all the fat, and, when it is cold, break it with whites of eggs as you do other jelly. Put part of it into a pan or mould that will hold the turkey, and, when it is cold, lay the turkey upon it with the breast downward; then cover it with the rest of the jelly. When you serve it, turn it out whole upon the dish.

Roasted Turkey, delicate Gravy for.

Prepare a very rich brown gravy with truffles cut in it; slit the skins off some chesnuts with a knife, and fry them in butter till thoroughly done, but not burned, and serve them whole in the sauce. There may be a few sausages about the turkey.

Turkey or Veal stuffing.

Mix a quarter of a pound of beef suet, the same quantity of bread crumbs, two drachms of parsley, a drachm and a half of sweet marjoram, or lemon-thyme, and the same of grated lemon-peel; an onion or shalot chopped fine, a little salt and pepper, and the yolks of two eggs, all pounded well together. For a boiled turkey, add the soft part of a dozen oysters, a little grated ham or tongue, and an anchovy, if you please.

GAME.

Hare, to dress.

STUFF and lard the hare, trussing it as for roasting: put it into a fish-kettle, with two quarts of strong beef gravy, one of red wine, a bunch of sweet-herbs, some slices of lemon, pepper, salt, a few cloves, and a nutmeg. Cover it up close, and let it simmer over a slow fire till three parts done. Take it up, put it into a dish, and strew over it crumbs of bread, a few sweet-herbs chopped fine, some grated lemon-peel, and half a nutmeg. Set it before the fire, and baste it till it is of a fine light brown; and, while it is doing, skim the gravy, thicken it with the yolk of an egg and a piece of butter rolled in flour, and, when done, put it in a dish, and the rest in a boat or terrine.

Hare, to roast.

Take half a pint of cream, grate bread into it; a little winter savory, thyme, and parsley; shred these very fine; half a nutmeg grated, and half of the hare's liver, shred; beat an egg, yolk and white together, and mix it in with it, and half a spoonful of flour if you think it too light. Put it into the hare and sew it up. Have a quart of cream to baste it with. When the hare is roasted, take some of the best of the cream out of the dripping-pan, and make it fine and smooth by beating it with a spoon. Have ready melted a little thick butter, and mix it with the cream, and a little of the pudding out of the hare's belly, as much as will make it thick.

Another way.

Lard the hare well with bacon; make a pudding of grated bread, and chop small the heart and liver, parboiled, with beef-suet and sweet-herbs. With the marrow mix some eggs, spice, and cream; then sew it in the belly of the hare; roast, and serve it up with butter, drawn with cream, gravy, or claret.

Hare, to hash.

Cut the hare into small pieces, and, if any stuffing is left, rub it small in gravy, and put to it a glass of red wine, a little pepper, salt, an onion, and a slice of lemon. Toss it up till hot through, and then take out the lemon and onion.

Hare, to jug. No. 1.

Cut and put it into a jug, with the same ingredients as for stewing, but no water or beer; cover it closely; set it in a kettle of boiling water, and keep it boiling three hours, or until the hare is tender; then pour your gravy into the stewpan, and put to it a glass of red wine and a little cayenne; but if necessary put a little more of the gravy, thicken it with flour; boil it up; pour it over the hare, and add a little lemon-juice.

Hare, to jug. No. 2.

Cut and joint the hare into pieces; scald the liver and bruise it with a spoon; mix it with a little beaten mace, grated lemon-peel, pepper, salt, thyme, and parsley shred fine, and a whole onion stuck with a clove or two; lay the head and neck at the bottom of the jar; lay on it some seasoning, a very thin slice of fat bacon, then some hare, and bacon, seasoned well in. Stop close the jug or jar with a cork, to prevent any water getting in or the steam evaporating; set it in a pot of hot water, and let it boil three hours; then have ready some strong beef gravy boiling, and pour it into the jug till the hare is just covered; shake it, pour it into your dish, and take out the onion.

Hare, to jug. No. 3.

Cut the hare in pieces, but do not wash it; season with an onion shred fine, a bunch of sweet-herbs, such as thyme, parsley, sweet marjoram, and the peel of one lemon. Cut half a pound of fat bacon into thin slices; then put it into a jug, first a layer of hare and then one of bacon; proceed thus till the jug is full: stop it close, that no steam may escape; then put it in a pot of boiling water, and let it boil three hours. Take up the jug; put in a quarter of a pound of butter mixed with flour; set it in your kettle again for a quarter of an hour, then put it in your dish. Garnish with lemon-peel.

Hare, to jug. No. 4.

Cut the hare in pieces, and half season and lard them. Put the hare into a large-mouthed jug, with two onions stuck with cloves, and a faggot of sweet-herbs; close down, and let it boil three hours. Take it out, and serve up hot.

Hare, to mince.

Boil the hare with onions, parsley, and apples, till tender; shred it small, and put in a pint of claret, a little pepper, salt, and nutmeg, with two or three anchovies, and the yolks of twelve eggs boiled hard and shred very small; stirring all well together. In serving up, put sufficient melted butter to make it moist. Garnish the dish with whites of eggs, cut in half, and some of the bones.

Hare, to stew.

Cut off the legs and shoulders, and cut out the back bone; cut into slices the meat that comes off the sides: put all these into a vessel with three quarters of a pint of small beer, the same of water, a large onion stuck with cloves, whole pepper, some salt, and a slice of lemon. Let this stew gently for an hour closely covered, and then put a quart of good gravy to it, stewing it gently two hours longer, till tender. Take out the hare, and rub half a spoonful of smooth flour in a little gravy; put it to the sauce and boil it up; add a little cayenne and salt if necessary; put in the hare, and, when hot through, serve it up in a terrine stand.

Hare stuffing.

Two ounces of beef suet, three ounces of bread crumbs, a drachm of parsley, half a drachm of shalot, the same of marjoram, lemon-thyme, grated lemon-peel, and two yolks of egg.

Partridge, to boil.

Cover them with water, and fifteen minutes will boil them. Sauce—celery, liver, mushroom, or onion sauces.

Partridge, to roast.

Half an hour will be sufficient; and for sauce, gravy and bread sauce.

Partridge à la Paysanne.

When you have picked and drawn them, truss and put them on a skewer, tie them to a spit, and lay them to roast. Put a piece of fat bacon on a toasting fork, and hold it over the birds, that as it melts it may drop upon them while roasting. After basting them well in this manner, strew over a few crumbs of bread and a little salt, cut fine some shalots, with a little gravy, salt and pepper, and the juice of half a lemon. Mix all these over the fire; thicken them up; pour them into a dish, and lay your partridges upon them.

Partridge à la Polonaise.

Pick and draw a brace of partridges, and put a piece of butter in their bellies; nut them on the spit, and cover them with slices of bacon, and over that with paper, and lay them down to a moderate fire. While roasting, cut same shalots and parsley very small; mix these together, adding slices of ginger with pepper and salt; take a piece of butter, and work them up into a stiff paste. When the birds are nearly done, take them up; gently raise the wings and legs, and under each put a piece of paste; then hold them tight together, and squeeze over them a little orange juice and a good deal of zest from the peel. Serve them up hot with good gravy.

Partridge à la Russe.

Pick, draw, and cut into quarters some young partridges, and put them into white wine; set a stewpan with melted bacon over a brisk fire; then put your partridges in, turning them two or three times. Add a glass of brandy; set them over a slow fire, and, when they have stewed some time, put in a few mushrooms cut into slices, with good gravy. Simmer them briskly, and skim the fat off as it rises. When done, put in a piece of butter rolled in flour, and squeeze in the juice of lemon.

Partridge rolled.

Lard some young partridges with ham and bacon, and strew over some salt and pepper, with beaten mace, sweet-herbs cut small, and some shred lemon-peel. Take some thin beef steaks, taking care that they have no holes in them, and strew over some seasoning, squeezing over some lemon-juice. Lay a partridge upon each steak, roll it up, and tie it round to keep it together, and pepper the outside. Set on a stewpan, with some slices of bacon and an onion cut in pieces; then carefully lay the partridges in, put some rich gravy to them, and stew gently till they are done. Take the partridges out of the beef; lay them in a dish, and pour over them some rich essence of ham.

Partridge stewed.

Stuff the craws with bread crumbs, grated lemon-peel, a bit of butter, shalot chopped, parsley, nutmeg, salt and pepper, and yolk of egg; rub the inside with pepper and salt. Half roast them; then stew them with rich gravy and a little Madeira, a piece of lemon-peel, an onion, savory, and spice, if necessary, for about half an hour. Take out the lemon-peel and onion, and thicken with a little flour; garnish with hard yolks of eggs; add artichoke bottoms boiled and quartered.

Salme of Partridges.

Cut up the partridges neatly into wings, legs, and breast; keep the backs and rumps apart to put into sauce; take off all the skin very clean, so that not a bit remains; then pare them all round, put them in a stewpan, with a little jelly gravy, just to cover them; heat them thoroughly, taking care they do not burn; strain off the gravy, and leave the partridge in the pan away from the fire, covering the pan. Take a large onion, three or four slices of ham, free from all fat, one carrot, cut in dice, a dessert-spoonful of mushrooms, clear washed from vinegar if they are pickled, two cloves, a little parsley and thyme, and a bit of butter, of the size of a walnut; fry these lightly; add a glass and a half of white wine, together with the jelly in which the partridges were heated, and as much more as will make up a pint of rich sauce, thickened with a little flour and butter; put in the parings of the birds except the claws; let them stew for an hour and a half on the corner of the stove; skim very clear; put in one lump of sugar, and strain the whole through a sieve; put the saucepan containing the partridges in boiling water, till thoroughly heated; lay the different parts of the birds neatly in a very hot dish; pour the sauce over them; have some slices of bread cut oval, rather broad at one end, neatly fried; lay them round the dish, and serve up.

Partridge, to pot.

For two brace of partridges take a small handful of salt, and of pepper, mace, and cloves, a quarter of an ounce each. With these, when well mixed, rub the birds thoroughly, inside and outside. Take a large piece of butter, season it well, put it into them, and lay them in pots, with the breasts downward. The pots must be large enough to admit the butter to cover them while they bake. Set them in a moderate oven; let them stand two hours; then take them out, and let them well drain from the gravy. Put them again into the pots; clear the butter in which they were baked through a sieve, and fill up the pots with it.

Partridge Pie.

Bone your partridges, and stuff them with forcemeat, made of breast of chicken and veal, ham and beef-suet, all chopped very fine, but not pounded in a mortar, which would spoil it. Season with mace, pepper, salt, a very little shalot, and lemon-peel. Put the whole into a stewpan; keep it stirred; add three eggs; have a raised crust, and lay thin slices of good fat bacon at the bottom and all round.

Pheasant, to boil.

Boil the birds in abundance of water; if they are large, they will require three quarters of an hour; if small, about half an hour. For sauce—stewed white celery, thickened with cream, and a bit of butter rolled in flour; pour this over them.

Pheasant, with white sauce.

Truss the bird with the legs inward, (like a fowl for boiling); singe it well; take a little butter and the fat of some bacon, and fry the pheasant white; when sufficiently firm, take it out of the pan; then put a spoonful of flour into the butter; fry this flour white; next add a pint of veal or game jelly; put in a few mushrooms, if pickled to be well washed; cut small a bunch of parsley, a large onion, a little thyme, one clove, a pinch of salt, cayenne pepper, and a small lump of sugar; stew the bird in this sauce till done; this may be known by putting a fork into the flesh, and seeing that no blood issues out; then skim off the fat and drain the pheasant; then strain and boil the gravy in which it has been stewed; have ready a few mushrooms fried white in butter; then thicken the gravy with the yolk of four eggs and two table-spoonfuls of cream, throw in the mushrooms, place the pheasant in a hot dish, pour the sauce over it, and serve it up.